INDIANA BELIEVER

30 DAYS OF DEVOTIONS FOR THE HOOSIER FOOTBALL FAITHFUL

DEL DUDUIT

Birmingham, Alabama

Indiana Believer

Iron Stream
An imprint of Iron Stream Media
100 Missionary Ridge
Birmingham, AL 35242
IronStreamMedia.com

Library of Congress Control Number: 2026938431

Cover design by twolineSTUDIO.com

ISBN: 978-1-56309-813-0 (paperback)
ISBN: 978-1-56309-814-7 (eBook)

1 2 3 4 5—30 29 28 27 26

"The 2025 Hoosier football season was an inspiration. Not only to their fans but to an entire nation. There is much we can learn from this real-life Cinderella story. Their success has been celebrated, commemorated, documented, and commented on by sports pundits. But there's more to the story. The principles of success are universal and immutable. They apply in competition, business, relationships, and our daily living. With his many books featuring stories of how athletes from a variety of sports have found the inner strength that fueled their drive to excellence, Del Duduit connects how their spiritual lives are at the foundation of their achievement. The same truths are available to each of us. Like the rest of his books, each chapter in Indiana Believer will help you trace the fruits of winning to their roots in biblical truth." —**Mark "Coach" Prasek**, founder of PJNET.tv

"As a former Big Ten football player with the University of Michigan, I know how hard it is to win at the highest level. As a pastor of a church and a father, I am familiar with what it takes to be a spiritual leader. And as a football fan in general, I am aware of the dedication that is needed to be successful. In this book, Del Duduit takes an exciting program like the Hoosiers, and uses the success it has experienced to motivate the reader to follow Christ to be a winner in life. Although I am true to the Maize and Blue, I found Indiana Believer to be a book I can relate to and be inspired by all season long." —**Cyle Young**, pastor and author

"I love this book because each chapter is an excellent example of how sports goes hand-in-hand with everyday life and one's faith in a process. For example, the 73-0 win over Indiana State was one that really stood out to me, because even though Fernando Mendoza went nineteen of twenty passing, he said that his decision-making still needed work and improvement. This shows greatness as Mendoza is never looking to settle, which is a big reason why he's considered to be a high NFL draft pick. However, how Del applied it is brilliant because it goes back to details and the attention we put into the processes with everything that we do. That goes back to faith. If we apply a trust and belief factor into following God to answer our prayers, and trust His timing, that then parlays. And even if it doesn't parlay into how we foresee it, that's because God has a greater plan for us, whether that's playing sports, working in sports, or doing something else. At the end of the day, Del's message, to me, is all about serving a calling and a purpose that is bigger than you by believing in God and trusting in Him to provide you with answers over a long period of time, even if those answers may not make sense to us. —**Kevin Colley**, sports editor, PDT/HD Media

Other Books by Del Duduit

Alabama Devotions
Auburn Devotions
Florida Devotions
Florida State Devotions
Sports Shorts
Buckeye Believer

The Stars of the Faith Series

Dugout Devotions
First Down Devotions
Dugout Devotions II
First Down Devotions II
Birdies, Bogeys, and Blessings
Goal Line Devotions
Bengal Believer
Fierce
Fútbol Faith

This book is dedicated to the memory and life of my nephew, Josh, who loved all sports and family and was a joy to be around. You are missed.

CONTENTS

ACKNOWLEDGMENTS

I'd like to thank the following for all they did to make the book a reality.

1. My publisher at Iron Stream Media—John Herring.
2. My editor—Susan Cornell.
3. My team at ISM—Michele Trumble and Kim McCulla.
4. My agent—Cyle Young.
5. My wife—Angie Duduit.

DAY 1

SHIFT THE MOMENTUM

August 30, 2025: Indiana 27, Old Dominion 14

For God alone, O my soul, wait in silence,
for my hope is from him.
He only is my rock and my salvation,
my fortress; I shall not be shaken.

—Psalm 62:5–6

The season opener at Memorial Stadium in Bloomington, Indiana, set the tone for the entire season. The No. 20 Hoosiers had to overcome a slow start to knock off Old Dominion for Indiana's thirteenth straight nonconference home-opening win.

Old Dominion stunned the Hoosiers when quarterback Colton Joseph bolted seventy-five yards for a touchdown and grabbed an early 7–0 lead. But with about a minute left in the first quarter, Indiana's Jonathan Brady returned a punt ninety-one yards to tie the game 7–7. That play gave the Hoosiers the boost they needed to shift the momentum in their favor.

From that point on, Indiana would pour it on Old Dominion. A Nico Radicic twenty-two-yard field goal followed by a Fernando Mendoza five-yard touchdown run gave IU a 17–7 lead at halftime.

Kaelon Black blasted through for a two-yard touchdown run and then Radicic booted a twenty-five-yard field goal for the 27–7 lead. Indiana struggled at first on the offensive end and had issues scoring in the red zone. But Brady came through with the punt return for the score at the right time to shift the momentum for the Hoosiers.

> *And let us consider how to stir up one another to love and good works, not neglecting to meet together, as is the habit of some, but encouraging one another, and all the more as you see the Day drawing near.*
>
> —Hebrews 10:24–25

FOR THE CREAM AND CRIMSON

Are you behind on the scoreboard and need something to change in your life? Are you in a spiritual rut? It happens. It's nothing to be ashamed of but can cause you to fumble in the red zone if it's not addressed. Are you in need of a momentum-shifting play in your life?

HOO-HOO-HOO-HOOSIERS!

You can shift the momentum in your daily life by anchoring in spiritual disciplines. This might sound difficult, but it's not. You can make the shift to cultivate a proactive mindset and engage in actions that produce purpose and meaning. Key fundamental methods include daily repentance and Bible study. This will create a deeper connection with your church community and will encourage you to seek miracles through prayer. It will also help you to forgive those who have hurt you and to bring closure to conflicts. It's a win-win. Here are some key factors to shift the momentum in your favor.

1. Repent often. Look at repentance as an act of joy instead of a burden. When you recognize that you are weak and He is strong, then that will strengthen your faith. Don't dread repentance but instead look at it as the medicine that will make you better. "The Lord is not slow to fulfill his promise as some count slowness, but is patient toward you, not wishing that any should perish, but that all should reach repentance" (2 Peter 3:9).

2. Expect a miracle. When you cultivate and grow your faith through prayer and Bible study, your fears will fade into hope. You must be patient in this step and not test God. For example, you should not hope and pray that the Lord will deposit $1 million in your bank account tomorrow, but you should trust that He will provide your needs. "But seek first the kingdom of God and his righteousness, and all these things will be added to you" (Matthew 6:33).

3. Put an end to conflicts. You can forgive and reach out to those you have an issue with. When you hold on to pain, it festers and produces bitterness. End the conflict

and find your peace through His grace. "And if he sins against you seven times in the day, and turns to you seven times, saying, 'I repent,' you must forgive him" (Luke 17:4).

4. Serve others. When you take part in charitable acts and volunteer work to demonstrate the love of Christ in you, that shifts the focus to others. You are out of the spotlight and others are the center of attention. Do this without posting pictures or bragging to your friends. "For you were called to freedom, brothers. Only do not use your freedom as an opportunity for the flesh, but through love serve one another" (Galatians 5:13).

5. Share your story. You can do this in a wide variety of ways. You can chat about your experience at church over the weekend at lunch with your colleagues; you can share your thoughts on social media; you can post your devotion to the Savior on your social media profile or even blog about it for others to read. The point here is to let everyone know you are a believer.

When you take the time to focus on these suggestions, you will shift the momentum back in the right direction. You don't have to bombard those around you with spiritual conversations all the time and turn people off, but you can let everyone know how you feel at appropriate times and set the tone. The right testimony at the right time can be the punt return for a TD that you need. One play can make the difference.

DAY 2

THE LORD WILL PROVIDE

September 6, 2025: Indiana 56, Kennesaw State 9

Consider the ravens: they neither sow nor reap, they have neither storehouse nor barn, and yet God feeds them. Of how much more value are you than the birds!

—Luke 12:24

The No. 23 Hoosiers hosted Kennesaw State and quickly took care of business on Saturday, September 6, at Merchants Bank Field at Memorial Stadium in Bloomington. The game was less a contest and more an early statement that Indiana football was to be reckoned with and respected.

Running back Riley Nowakowski put the Hoosiers on the board with a one-yard plunge into the end zone with 8:28 left in the first quarter. Indiana added to its lead about five minutes later when quarterback Fernando Mendoza connected with Elijah Sarratt on a nine-yard TD strike for the 14–0 lead.

With 3:40 to go in the second quarter, Lee Beebe Jr. broke through and scampered eleven yards for the touchdown and the 21–3 lead after Nico Radicic's point after kick. Kennesaw was able to boot two more field goals to cut the deficit to 21–9, but that would be all the scoring they would do, because the Hoosiers poured it on the visiting team.

Mendoza connected with Sarratt again for a three-yard TD pass, followed by a seventy-five-yard romp for a touchdown by Omar Cooper. The duo of Mendoza and Sarratt kept the heat on as they made good on a twenty-yard TD pass for the 42–9 lead. The amazing QB fired two more TD passes to end the game, with one going to E. J. Williams for an eight-yard score and the next one going to Charlie Becker for a six-yard touchdown and the final 56–9 lead.

After the game, Indiana head coach Curt Cignetti told IUHoosiers.com that the second win of the season sent a statement. "Good day," he said. "I think we made the improvement we needed to make, but it's far from perfect. . . . But we took a step forward with the step we needed to take."[1]

What do you need from the Lord?

> *And God is able to make all grace abound to you, so that having all sufficiency in all things at all times, you may abound in every good work.*
>
> —2 Corinthians 9:8

FOR THE CREAM AND CRIMSON

You are also not perfect but you need to move forward in your Christian journey. If you are not going ahead, then you are

1 "Postgame Quotes: Kennesaw State," Indiana University Athletics, September 6, 2025, https://iuhoosiers.com/news/2025/9/6/football-postgame-quotes-kennesaw-state.

moving backward. Your needs are basic but unique to you. Perhaps you need a new job or a new beginning. Maybe you need clarity on a relationship or guidance on how to raise your children. Or maybe you need God to provide healing or to show up and provide reassurance. Needs are endless. If you are honest, some days are harder than others and discouragement can be real.

HOO-HOO-HOO-HOOSIERS!

No matter the need, God will provide and allow you to move forward. When you lack encouragement or are facing a financial giant or a medical mountain, the Lord has promised to be with you. When there are intense trials you have to face and obstacles you have to battle, you must know His love for you is endless. There may be times you don't notice it, and that is exactly what the devil wants you to do in those moments. But have confidence that He will provide for you. Here are some ways God will give you exactly what you need.

1. He gives mercy. His mercy is unconditional love and compassion. You deserve His wrath and judgment, but through the sacrifice of the Son, you are spared from eternal torture and granted life everlasting. His mercy is wonderful and should never be taken for granted. "For judgment is without mercy to one who has shown no mercy. Mercy triumphs over judgment" (James 2:13).

2. He gives grace. This is unmerited favor and goodwill in your life. It's a free gift and represents goodness,

opportunity, and salvation. You cannot live a successful Christian life without God's grace. "But he gives more grace. Therefore it says, 'God opposes the proud but gives grace to the humble'" (James 4:6).

3. He gives healing. God can heal your life of sin and restore your soul. He can grant physical healing from an illness as well as spiritual and emotional healing. "He heals the brokenhearted / and binds up their wounds" (Psalm 147:3).

4. He gives forgiveness. This is unexplainable. Forgiveness is a beautiful gift to receive. It can restore relationships and be the very thing you need in your life. You might need to be on the giving end of forgiveness or on the receiving end. Give it freely to those who hurt you, and the Lord will provide your needs.

5. He gives peace. There is no better feeling in the world than to have peace of mind. The Lord is the only one who can give this to you. Peace will not come in the form of a new job or a touchdown on a big play. Those things can make you happy, but they cannot provide peace. "In peace I will both lie down and sleep; / for you alone, O Lord, make me dwell in safety" (Psalm 4:8).

You, like the Hoosiers football team, are not perfect. But you can move forward knowing the Lord provides all your needs. You just have to accept them and not ask any questions. Be grateful for mercy, grace, healing, forgiveness, and peace.

DAY 3

MAKE BETTER DECISIONS

September 12, 2025: Indiana 73, Indiana State 0

Though he fall, he shall not be cast headlong,
for the L*ORD* *upholds his hand.*

—Psalm 37:24

Indiana quarterback Fernando Mendoza was about as good as you can get on Merchants Bank Field at Memorial Stadium. The signal-caller finished the game with 270 yards passing with five touchdowns and nineteen of twenty passes completed. And this was done in the first half alone. He didn't even play in the final two quarters as IU walloped Indiana State 73–0.

Mendoza was *almost* perfect, as only one pass did not connect with a receiver. "There's a lot of stuff I have to improve on," Mendoza said in a recap from IUHoosiers.com. "Although the score might not look like it and the stat line might not look like it, there are a lot of things I have to clean up. I need to have better footwork. I need to be smarter in my decision making."[2]

---

2 "Hoosiers Dominant in Record-Setting Win Over Indiana State," Indiana University Athletics, September 12, 2025, https://iuhoosiers.com/news/2025/9/12/football-hoosiers-dominant-in-record-setting-win-over-indiana-state.

Can that attitude apply to you? Can you be smarter in making life decisions? Of course you can.

Mendoza completed 95 percent of his passes that game—a number that is unheard of in Division I or even NFL ranks. But he wanted it all—he wanted to be perfect. In the end he was not Superman but a mere human being and athlete.

Trust in the LORD with all your heart,
and do not lean on your own understanding.
In all your ways acknowledge him,
and he will make straight your paths.
—Proverbs 3:5–6

FOR THE CREAM AND CRIMSON

You are faced with hundreds of choices every single day in life. According to research from *Psychology Today*, you will make about thirty-five thousand decisions in twenty-four hours.[3] Most of them are routine, such as what time to get out of bed, what to have for breakfast, what to wear for the day, what to entertain yourself with, who to talk to, what to say, when to check emails, what to purchase, what route to take when you travel, and so on. You get the idea. But there are also more complex decisions to make such as budgeting choices, what career path to take, who to marry or date, when to seek medical care, how to manage your time, or what church to attend. Life is full of decisions. Every

3 Eva M. Krockow, "How Many Decisions Do We Make Each Day?," *Psychology Today*, September 27, 2018, https://www.psychologytoday.com/us/blog/stretching-theory/201809/how-many-decisions-do-we-make-each-day.

day features a barrage of choices. What choices do you have to make?

HOO-HOO-HOO-HOOSIERS!

Your decision list might be huge and complicated, or it may be short and simple for the day. How do you make your choices? Do you just know, or do you ask for advice and help from friends and family? Do you think you can make a major decision alone, or do you consult the heavenly Father in these matters? Do you even think to pray about it? Will you be humble enough to listen? Do you take into consideration how your choice will impact those around you? Here are some things to consider when you are faced with a tougher decision than if you should have that second cup of coffee in the morning. (And, by the way, that's a no-brainer.)

1. Commit to prayer. That sounds basic but it's at times a last priority. Pray at every stage—before, during, and after a decision—to ask for wisdom, alignment with God's will, and peace. Pray before you submit the job application. Pray before you ask a person out on a date. Pray before you go into the doctor's office. Then comes the hard part: listen and obey. "Commit your work to the LORD, / and your plans will be established" (Proverbs 16:3).

2. Seek counsel. Don't just ask within your inner circle for a rubber stamp of approval. Talk to your pastor or therapist or someone within your community whom you respect and who has earned life scars. In the end,

it's your choice, but it's always wise to gain perspective from others. "Without counsel plans fail, / but with many advisers they succeed" (Proverbs 15:22).

3. Examine your motives. Why do you want that job? Why do you want to go out on that date? What do you hope to accomplish? Will your decision be in touch with God's priorities in your life? Will it improve your spiritual relationship with Him, or is it all about you? What is your motivation? "I know, my God, that you test the heart and have pleasure in uprightness. In the uprightness of my heart I have freely offered all these things, and now I have seen your people, who are present here, offering freely and joyously to you" (1 Chronicles 29:17).

4. List out the pros and cons. This is a good idea in most choices. If the pros outnumber the cons, then it might be a good choice. Be honest about this list and look at the good, the bad, and the ugly.

5. Will your choice glorify the Lord? If it does not, then rethink your options. If God opens the door, then go through it. If He closes the door, don't force it open. "So, whether you eat or drink, or whatever you do, do all to the glory of God" (1 Corinthians 10:31).

You can make better, God-honoring decisions by anchoring choices in prayer, scripture, and wise counsel. The key steps include asking the Lord for guidance and for wisdom and for courage to make a final decision. If you aim to glorify the Lord in all you do, then you will complete all your pass attempts in life, no matter the score or if it's a big touchdown.

DAY 4

MAKE A STATEMENT

September 20, 2025: Indiana 63, Illinois 10

Come and hear, all you who fear God,
and I will tell what he has done for my soul.
—Psalm 66:16

By now, the Hoosiers had everyone's attention. After they thumped Big Ten rival Illinois 63–10 on a Saturday night, the college football world did a double take. "Are these guys for real?"

On a nationally televised game, Indiana football made the statement that they are the real deal. The No. 19 Indiana Hoosiers had no problems cruising to the win over a veteran top-10 team in Illinois, who had aspirations themselves of a College Football Playoff selection. But IU had other plans.

Quarterback Fernando Mendoza was lights out on fire. He completed twenty-one of twenty-three pass attempts for 267 yards with five touchdowns and no interceptions in just three quarters. Defensive cornerback D'Angelo Ponds, a standout on the corner, set the tone for the Hoosiers when he scored on a blocked punt and returned the ball eleven yards into the end zone. After Mendoza connected with Omar Cooper for an eleven-yard TD strike, the rout was on.

After the game, Ponds hit the nail on the head. "This was our first Big Ten game," he said in an article in IUHoosiers.com. "We wanted to make a statement. We did that. It shows how dominant we can be. We deserve to be in the top 10. I feel we proved that."[4]

Do you need to prove you are a believer? How do you do that?

> *So everyone who acknowledges me before men, I also will acknowledge before my Father who is in heaven.*
>
> —Matthew 10:32

FOR THE CREAM AND CRIMSON

Do your colleagues at work know you are a Christian? Do the friends you hang out with know this as well? How about your family? If you have children, do they have any idea? Telling people in your life that you love God is one thing—but showing it is another. Many athletes may point to the heavens after a fantastic play for everyone to see, but do they live the life in private? Do you?

---

4 Pete DiPrimio, "Hoosiers Earn Top-10 Win over Illini," Indiana University Athletics, September 20, 2025, https://iuhoosiers.com/news/2025/9/20/football-hoosiers-make-statement-against-no-9-illinois.

HOO-HOO-HOO-HOOSIERS!

In today's world, people become offended easily if your opinion doesn't match theirs. Does this intimidate you? Does it cause you not to want to share your beliefs with them? Are you in fear of losing your job or a lawsuit for proclaiming the good news? This is real and has to be taken into consideration at times. But you also need to make a statement that you are a follower of Jesus Christ. Here are some ways you can do that.

1. Everyday conversation. Words matter. Work into a conversation that you attended church over the weekend or that your kids had a wonderful time at a youth camp. You can have a chat without being obnoxious or judgmental, but at the same time you can let others know you have a grounded faith. Use appropriate language and be above obscene words. "I tell you, on the day of judgment people will give account for every careless word they speak, for by your words you will be justified, and by your words you will be condemned" (Matthew 12:36–37).

2. Simple lifestyle. You can live a comfortable life without flaunting any success you have. It's OK to have things, but make sure you stay grounded in a fundamental lifestyle of gratitude. If you are on the other end of this, show humility and not anger or jealousy. Be happy and content with what God has given to you.

3. Actions. Show kindness and love toward others. Don't use foul language or make crude gestures in public. Volunteer and help those in need. "In all things I have shown you that by working hard in this way we must help the weak and remember the words of the Lord Jesus, how he himself said, 'It is more blessed to give than to receive'" (Acts 20:35).

4. How you present yourself with attire. If you feel comfortable, wear a cross necklace or a tie with a Christian message on it or a T-shirt people can read.

5. Visuals. Don't be ashamed to pray over a meal in public or attend a Christian concert in an auditorium. Have your Bible out for your coworkers or family to see when they pass by (and don't forget to read it too). Have a coffee mug with your favorite scripture displayed. "For whoever is ashamed of me and of my words, of him will the Son of Man be ashamed when he comes in his glory and the glory of the Father and of the holy angels" (Luke 9:26).

The Hoosiers made a statement when they defeated conference foe Illinois. Up to that point in the season, some skeptics might have thought that Indiana was just playing some weaker opponents. But the college football world was about to be introduced to Hoosier football. Everyone knew they were for real. Are you?

DAY 5

COME BACK FROM YOUR PAST

September 27, 2025: Indiana 20, Iowa 15

In him we have redemption through his blood, the forgiveness of our trespasses, according to the riches of his grace.

—Ephesians 1:7

For the first time in the 2025 season, the Indiana Hoosiers were tested. After four blowout wins, IU found itself in a contested battle. Quarterback Fernando Mendoza was chased, knocked down, hit hard, and even bloodied a time or two during the game.

With 1:28 to go in regulation, the Iowa defense blitzed Mendoza, who showed courage under pressure and delivered a forty-nine-yard touchdown strike to Elijah Sarratt to keep the eleventh-ranked Hoosiers undefeated at 5–0 overall and 2–0 in the Big Ten Conference.

"We did what we needed to do," defensive lineman Stephen Daley said after the game in a report from IUHoosiers.com. "At big moments, big-time players make big-time plays."[5]

---

5 Pete DiPrimio, "First Road Test Passed," Indiana University Athletics, September 27, 2025, https://iuhoosiers.com/news/2025/9/27/football-hoosiers-pass-first-road-test-against-hawkeyes-pete.

Mendoza completed thirteen of twenty-three passes for 233 yards and two TDs, but he did throw his first interception of the season. Sarratt grabbed six catches for 133 yards, which included the stunning game-winning catch. The Hoosiers had their backs up against the wall and made the comeback. What have you had to come back from in life?

In whom we have redemption, the forgiveness of sins.
—Colossians 1:14

FOR THE CREAM AND CRIMSON

You may find yourself in a desperate fight to stay undefeated in life. You may be cruising along with no issues when you suddenly find yourself behind on the scoreboard with time running out. How do you respond? Perhaps you've been chased and knocked down, hit hard by the devil, and even bloodied a time or two. Do you have the courage to stand in the pocket and deliver the touchdown pass against all odds?

HOO-HOO-HOO-HOOSIERS!

The comeback is easier said than done. As a follower of Christ, you can come back from bad choices and the past by sincerely repenting, confessing to God, and accepting His forgiveness to move forward. Sounds easy, right? In theory it is. But you, as a human created by the Lord, will complicate things. Here are some ways to make the comeback pass and stay undefeated.

1. No excuses. You are responsible for what you do—period. There may be circumstances that may have influenced what you did, but you did it in the end. You knew right from wrong. The devil will disguise it and make you the victim when in fact it's all on you. Own it. "So then each of us will give an account of himself to God" (Romans 14:12).

2. Accept His forgiveness. God has offered forgiveness if you ask and mean what you tell Him. His forgiveness is free but not without a cost. His Son paid the price for you. Accept the forgiveness offered. "If we confess our sins, he is faithful and just to forgive us our sins and to cleanse us from all unrighteousness. If we say we have not sinned, we make him a liar, and his word is not in us" (1 John 1:9–10).

3. Forgive yourself. This can be a tough one. You may hold yourself to a higher standard and be disappointed in your past. But once the Lord has forgiven you, then you need to do the same. If others don't, then that's on them. Take responsibility and realize you are valuable in God's eye. "I acknowledged my sin to you, / and I did not cover my iniquity; / I said, 'I will confess my transgressions to the LORD,' / and you forgave the iniquity of my sin. Selah" (Psalm 32:5).

4. Learn from mistakes. There is always a lesson to learn. When you look at the damage your actions may have caused, vow to never let that happen again. Your mistakes are not a life sentence, and they are never too

big for God to overcome. "Do not be conformed to this world, but be transformed by the renewal of your mind, that by testing you may discern what is the will of God, what is good and acceptable and perfect" (Romans 12:2).

5. Don't look back. Rooster Cogburn (John Wayne) once said that "looking back is a bad habit."[6] Mendoza would not have completed the game-winning TD if he had thrown the ball backward. Go forward and don't allow the devil to bring up your past.

Maybe you have moved on from something in your past, and that's fantastic. But if you are like a lot of others who have sinned and think no one loves you, then you are not alone. This is a trap set by the devil to keep you down and hand you the loss. Break the chains and move forward in your Christian journey to stay unbeaten. You can face challenges and come away with the win.

---

6 *True Grit*, directed by Henry Hathaway (Paramount Pictures, 1969).

DAY 6

IT'S FUN BUT NOT EASY

October 11, 2025: Indiana 30, Oregon 20

Trust in the L*ORD with all your heart,*
and do not lean on your own understanding.
—Proverbs 3:5

The Indiana Hoosiers believed it could happen, and it did. Indiana quarterback Fernando Mendoza didn't have his best game, but he guided the No. 7 Hoosiers to a huge 30–20 win at Oregon's Autzen Stadium on a Saturday afternoon. Mendoza finished with 215 yards passing and completed twenty of thirty-one passes with a crucial and rare interception in the fourth quarter.

But the Hoosiers believed in their ability and put ten points on the board in the final period to win on the road in a place where it's tough to get a victory. Indiana's win put the skids on Oregon's twenty-three-game regular season winning streak and an eighteen-game home winning streak.

"We never said it would be easy," Mendoza said. "We came in here, overcame adversity fantastically and rose to the moment. When the offense was on the field and we needed a game-winning drive, we did it. When the defense was on the field and we needed a stop, we got it."[7]

Being able to perform is one thing, but having trust in yourself and believing you can do it is another. The game was not an easy win, but after it was over, the fun started. Are you enjoying your Christian journey?

> *There is nothing better for a person than that he should eat and drink and find enjoyment in his toil. This also, I saw, is from the hand of God.*
>
> —Ecclesiastes 2:24

FOR THE CREAM AND CRIMSON

Life is meant to be enjoyed. But you will find difficulties along the way. You may encounter a bully who might make fun of you for your stance on faith. You might be subject to discrimination in the workplace or even threatened with punishment for your dedication to the Lord. You may have your social media accounts go black for some unknown reason, or the church you attend might be vandalized. It's unfortunate but it does happen.

HOO-HOO-HOO-HOOSIERS!

Do not be afraid or allow anyone to bully you. The Christian life is a fun journey, and you are allowed to enjoy yourself along the way. You must look at the persecution you may encounter as

7 Pete DiPrimio, "West Coast Win," Indiana University Athletics, October 11, 2025, https://iuhoosiers.com/news/2025/10/11/football-west-coast-win-PETE.

a speed bump. Ninety-five percent of the road is smooth while only about 5 percent is the bump. That's how you might view distractions along the way. If you do run over these speed bumps, take into consideration ways you can have fun while being a child of the King.

1. Attend fellowship events with others. Host a game night with fellow believers. Invite friends over for a meal or coffee to share stories and strengthen bonds. If you don't have a place that is suitable for this, organize one at someone else's place or go in together with some friends and rent a space. "For where two or three are gathered in my name, there am I among them" (Matthew 18:20).
2. Be creative. Journal your thoughts and compile what you write for later in life. Take up a fun hobby like painting or crafting or even host a faith-based podcast. Have fun. "And we know that for those who love God all things work together for good, for those who are called according to his purpose" (Romans 8:28).
3. Volunteer. You should consider this regardless. When you put the needs of others in front of your own, then you have the right frame of mind. God will reward that. "Therefore encourage one another and build one another up, just as you are doing" (1 Thessalonians 5:11).
4. Appreciate nature. Go on a hike or plan a trip to a destination full of God's wonderful handiwork. Take a stroll

in your yard at night and appreciate His marvelous creation in the heavens.

5. Maintain your positive outlook and attitude. This is essential. When you are faced with trials and uncomfortable situations, just know that He has a better plan for you. It's only temporary, and you will find victory in the end. "Keep your life free from love of money, and be content with what you have, for he has said, 'I will never leave you nor forsake you'" (Hebrews 13:5).

The Hoosiers knocked off the Ducks in a tough environment because they had to reach down and rely on determination in this win. You can do the same. The key is to have fun—even if you have to create it for yourself. The Christian life is the best one you can ask for. Don't get discouraged but rather rejoice because you already know the outcome that He has planned for you.

DAY 7

DEFENSE WINS GAMES

October 11, 2025: Indiana 30, Oregon 20

And you will know the truth, and the truth will set you free.

—John 8:32

This chapter is a piggyback from the last one. The game was vital and merits another one.

Indiana went into a traditionally hostile environment and came out victorious to keep their record perfect at 6–0 and 3–0 in the Big Ten Conference. Eugene, Oregon, is a tough place to play, but the Hoosiers dug down deep and went back to Bloomington, Indiana, with a much-needed and earned win.

The Hoosiers were tested but able to overcome obstacles and knocked off the Ducks 30–20, thanks in part to a stingy IU defense. Going into the matchup, Oregon averaged just over forty-six points per game. But when the game was over, the Ducks were held to thirteen offensive points, as their defense added one touchdown in the game.

When it came time to play, the Hoosiers were ready. "I liked our mindset going in," Indiana head coach Curt Cignetti said in an article published on IUHoosiers.com. "We were prepared to handle adversity. We handled it well and made the plays we had to make."[8]

Are you prepared for adversity? How will you respond when you go into hostile territory?

> *When the Spirit of truth comes, he will guide you into all the truth, for he will not speak on his own authority, but whatever he hears he will speak, and he will declare to you the things that are to come.*
>
> —John 16:13

FOR THE CREAM AND CRIMSON

If you have not been tested for your faith in Christ, rest assured you will be. You may have a relative or a colleague at work who will try to test your knowledge and make you defend why you are a believer. Chances are, those who question you are really searching for peace themselves. You have to be ready to defend yourself and your beliefs. The last thing you want to do is be unprepared to tell anyone why they should follow Christ. You need to be prepared and have the right mindset going in to come out a winner.

HOO-HOO-HOO-HOOSIERS!

Are you ready to answer questions like these? Why is there so much suffering in the world if God is a loving God? Where is

8 Pete DiPrimio, "West Coast Win," Indiana University Athletics, October 11, 2025, https://iuhoosiers.com/news/2025/10/11/football-west-coast-win-PETE.

your evidence that He is real? Why is there so much immorality in the church? Why does God remain hidden to the world? Why does the Bible contradict itself so much? Be prepared to hear it all and ready to give an answer. Remember that you might be the only Bible a person reads. Here are some ways to handle a tough environment and have your best defense on the field.

1. Don't argue. Listen to their point, even if you don't agree, and let them talk. However, don't allow them to be a bully. The last thing you want is a shouting match. If a conversation starts to be intense, walk away. Your reputation is more important than winning an argument. "Remind them of these things, and charge them before God not to quarrel about words, which does no good, but only ruins the hearers" (2 Timothy 2:14).

2. Know the truth. This will come in time and with steady Bible reading, devotions, and prayer. But if you know the facts—that Jesus was born of a virgin, lived a sinless life, was crucified and killed for your sins, rose to life after three days, and now reigns at the right hand of the Father—you are prepared. Teams win with a basic fundamental plan. If you are forgiven and a Christian, you're on the right path.

3. Stay centered in the gospel. Try not to sway into arenas that are away from the good news. Naysayers might want to talk about politics, sports, or current events. Those are fine, and you have an opinion like everyone

else. But what it all boils down to is the gospel. That should be your only defense. What does Scripture say? "For the word of God is living and active, sharper than any two-edged sword, piercing to the division of soul and of spirit, of joints and of marrow, and discerning the thoughts and intentions of the heart" (Hebrews 4:12).

4. Be honest. If you cannot explain something, then don't make it up. Simply say, "I don't know." "For we aim at what is honorable not only in the Lord's sight but also in the sight of man" (2 Corinthians 8:21).

5. Love them. This will catch any critic off guard. If you show them love and concern for their soul, then you might disarm them. It's hard to be angry with someone who shows love and kindness. Don't give in but rather stand higher. "All Scripture is breathed out by God and profitable for teaching, for reproof, for correction, and for training in righteousness, that the man of God may be complete, equipped for every good work" (2 Timothy 3:16–17).

The Hoosiers relied on their defense to boost their offensive performance to come out with the win in Oregon. They were ready to play and had the right mindset to play a tough opponent. You must be ready also. Remember that you are an ambassador for Christ. You are not perfect and might throw a pick-six like quarterback Fernando Mendoza did. But they responded and left victorious. You can too.

DAY 8

WATCH OUT FOR COMPLACENCY

October 18, 2025: Indiana 38, Michigan State 13

For the simple are killed by their turning away,
and the complacency of fools destroys them.

—Proverbs 1:32

The Indiana Hoosiers returned home from a big win on the West Coast and scored on their first five drives en route to a 38–13 drubbing of Michigan State.

The Spartans came into Merchants Bank Field in Bloomington hoping for a huge upset and even scored first on a field goal. But No. 3-ranked Indiana scored thirty-one straight points to stay undefeated at 7–0 overall and 4–0 in the Big Ten.

Quarterback Fernando Mendoza enjoyed a big day and threw for 332 yards and completed twenty-four of twenty-eight passes (85 percent) with four touchdowns, no sacks, and no interceptions. "We made a big emphasis to have a hot start," Mendoza said in an interview published by IUHoosiers.com. "You see teams come off a big win and be complacent. Coach [Curt] Cignetti made it a point throughout the week, never be complacent. Treat this team like every play is the game-winning play. We had that mindset."[9]

Are you complacent in your faith walk?

Because you have raged against me
and your complacency has come into my ears,
I will put my hook in your nose
and my bit in your mouth,
and I will turn you back on the way
by which you came.

—2 Kings 19:28

FOR THE CREAM AND CRIMSON

Complacency is a feeling of smug or uncritical satisfaction with yourself and your achievements. It's an attitude that says to everyone that you have arrived and can do no wrong. It can be easy for you to become complacent in your walk with Christ when every day is sunny and bright and without real problems. You may begin to think you have it all figured out and that God is just a genie in a bottle. But complacency is a dangerous thing. It can lead you to slowly drift away from God, and it can make you vulnerable to temptation.

---

9 Pete DiPrimio, "Spittoon Secured," Indiana University Athletics, October 18, 2025, https://iuhoosiers.com/news/2025/10/18/football-hoosiers-continue-to-roll-in-big-ten-showdown.

HOO-HOO-HOO-HOOSIERS!

Before you know it, complacency can creep into your life. It's characterized by a lack of zeal and spiritual stagnation. Over time you will show an indifference to the Lord and others in your life. You may never intend for this to happen, but it could. This is why you must be vigilant in your Christian walk. Here are some things to watch for to make sure you stay fresh and avoid becoming complacent.

1. When you give in to the "little" sins. When you lift your guard and begin accepting smaller sins as OK is one sign you are slipping into complacency. If God says it's wrong, then it's wrong. Who are you to judge or give a thumbs-up to sin because you want to be accepted or approved? You can love the sinner and hate the sin. "For what will it profit a man if he gains the whole world and forfeits his soul? Or what shall a man give in return for his soul?" (Matthew 16:26).

2. When you put more emphasis on convenience over obedience. When you begin to avoid situations that challenge your faith and go to where you are more comfortable, you might be complacent. An alcoholic probably should not go to bar and challenge his or her recovery, and you should not go where you are tempted. You are no match for the devil and his minions. "You have lived on the earth in luxury and in self-indulgence. You have fattened your hearts in a day of slaughter" (James 5:5).

3. When you neglect your alone time with God. The devil will put things in your life during your devotion times to see if you will take the bait. If you do not stick to your routine, you will push the Lord further and further away. Before you know it, you are out of touch and not spending the time you need for strength. If you are married and didn't talk to your spouse for several days, he or she may become concerned. Think how God feels when you put Him on a shelf. "How shall we escape if we neglect such a great salvation? It was declared at first by the Lord, and it was attested to us by those who heard" (Hebrews 2:3).

4. When you start to fade away from church. How successful would the Hoosiers be if they only showed up on game days without practicing? How successful will you be as a Christian if you don't go to church? You need to be there to become energized and hear the Word of God. If you are not fed by your church, then find one with a full spread. "Not neglecting to meet together, as is the habit of some, but encouraging one another, and all the more as you see the Day drawing near" (Hebrews 10:25).

5. When you are ungrateful. When you expect blessings in life and are not grateful for them, you might be complacent. You are not guaranteed anything in life. You have what you have due to God's grace. Show gratitude for everything, especially the little things. Why should the

> Lord grant you larger things in life if you don't show appreciation for the smaller ones?

Be careful not to get so caught up in chasing your personal goals that you allow it to overshadow what God has in store for you. If you isolate yourself from the Lord and still think you have it all under control, it will put you in a third-down with forty-five yards to go. Be aware of your situation and strive to stay close to His will for you.

DAY 9

STAY AWAY FROM TEMPTATION

October 25, 2025: Indiana 56, UCLA 6

No temptation has overtaken you that is not common to man. God is faithful, and he will not let you be tempted beyond your ability, but with the temptation he will also provide the way of escape, that you may be able to endure it.

—1 Corinthians 10:13

Indiana had no problem stopping UCLA's three-game winning streak at Memorial Stadium. The No. 3-ranked Hoosiers used a complete offensive attack combined with third-down efficiency and a relentless defense to improve to 8–0 on the season and 5–0 in the Big Ten. Quarterback Fernando Mendoza continued to amaze the college football world and completed fifteen of twenty-two passes for 168 yards and three touchdowns.

On the ground, Mendoza rushed for forty-five yards and added a TD. Overall, the ground game was in full force as the team rushed for 262 yards and one touchdown. The Hoosiers outgained the high-powered UCLA offense 476 to 201.

But the Indiana defense set the tone early when linebacker Aiden Fisher picked off a UCLA pass on the game's second play and rumbled twenty-five yards for the score. The IU defense was stingy, as the Bruins could only muster up fewer than ten yards on their first four drives and fumbled on the fifth. Isaiah Jones came into the game to replace an injured Fisher and piled up eight tackles.

The difference in the game was that UCLA could not get the Indiana offense off the field. It had no answer. At the same time, the Hoosier defense stymied UCLA's offense when it was fortunate enough to get the ball. Indiana had the ball for about twelve more minutes in the game.

What's your reaction when temptation comes your way?

> *Blessed is the man who remains steadfast under trial, for when he has stood the test he will receive the crown of life, which God has promised to those who love him. Let no one say when he is tempted, "I am being tempted by God," for God cannot be tempted with evil, and he himself tempts no one. But each person is tempted when he is lured and enticed by his own desire. Then desire when it has conceived gives birth to sin, and sin when it is fully grown brings forth death. Do not be deceived, my beloved brothers.*
>
> —James 1:12–16

FOR THE CREAM AND CRIMSON

It will happen. You will face temptation. The devil will make sure it doesn't avoid you. He's good at it and is aware of your weakness. You might face temptations of sexual sin, anger, pride, jealousy, lying, stealing, or some other area where Satan knows you might stumble.

HOO-HOO-HOO-HOOSIERS!

Being tempted is one thing and giving in is another. What is your weakness? You have one or two, if you're honest. Is it money? Is it lust? Perhaps you have a short fuse. Maybe it's alcohol or smoking. Do you crave attention or talk about people? No one is perfect, and the devil knows what buttons to push. Here are some ways you can deal with temptation.

1. Be honest with yourself. You have lived with yourself and know yourself well. You are aware of your likes and dislikes. You know what drives you to do what you do. You are human and have a corrupt nature. It's just the way you are. But you must know your enemy—and that is yourself. "To put off your old self, which belongs to your former manner of life and is corrupt through deceitful desires" (Ephesians 4:22).

2. Know your triggers. Temptation does not care what you think or do. It is a tool of the devil to lure you away from what you know is right. You want to give in to it because you believe and have been lied to that it will make you feel better. If you are bogged down with the sin of lust, don't see a movie that contains a lot of nudity. If you have a tendency for alcohol, stay away from the bar or liquor section of the grocery store.

3. Be accountable. There is no shame in sharing your struggles with those who face the same battles. There are support groups you can find and attend, or you can confide with a close friend or even your spouse. Be open and honest and don't look for a person who will approve of everything you want to do. Don't make excuses either. "Iron sharpens iron, / and one man sharpens another" (Proverbs 27:17).

4. Use the Word of God. Find a scripture verse you like and memorize it. When you are faced with temptation, quote it to yourself several times and just flee from the scene. You are no match for the devil. "Submit yourselves therefore to God. Resist the devil, and he will flee from you" (James 4:7).

5. Make sure you get rest. Temptation will present itself when you are at your weakest. Get enough daily rest. When you are tired, the devil will attack and make your weakness seem like a way to help you find peace. Don't fall for this trick. Your mind can be the devil's playground. "Put on the whole armor of God, that you may be able to stand against the schemes of the devil" (Ephesians 6:11).

Indiana's overall game plan was to dominate the Bruins, and it worked. The devil's plan for you and your future is total destruction. He will do it through any means necessary and does not play fair. Take heed and never entertain the attitude that you are untouchable.

DAY 10

WORKS WON'T GET YOU TO HEAVEN

November 1, 2025: Indiana 55, Maryland 10

For by grace you have been saved through faith. And this is not your own doing; it is the gift of God, not a result of works, so that no one may boast. For we are his workmanship, created in Christ Jesus for good works, which God prepared beforehand, that we should walk in them.

—Ephesians 2:8–10

The No. 2-ranked Hoosiers blasted Maryland 55–10 at College Park, Maryland. Indiana (9–0, 6–0) forced five Maryland turnovers and held the Terrapins to under fifty yards rushing for the entire game. According to an article published on IUHoosiers.com, this was the eighth consecutive game where the opponents were held to under one hundred yards rushing by the Hoosier defense.

The article continued: "It's hard to win on the road," Hoosier head coach Curt Cignetti said during a postgame radio show. "It was (Maryland's) Homecoming, a soldout crowd. They had a week off. They made a big play early with an interception and our defense did a great job to hold them to a field goal. Then the offense got rolling a little bit."[10]

That was an understatement because Indiana piled up fifty-five points and scored twenty unanswered points on four straight drives. Quarterback Fernando Mendoza completed fourteen of twenty-one passes for 201 yards with one touchdown and one interception. Even when the game as out of hand, the Hoosiers stuck with the game plan.

"I'm impressed with the way our guys listen to the message and play the way we want them to play," Cignetti continued. "That's a big part of it. Tomorrow is a new day. Everything is earned; nothing is given."

That's the perfect attitude in football but not in the Christian world. Nothing is earned. You cannot play your way into heaven.

> *But if it is by grace, it is no longer on the basis of works; otherwise grace would no longer be grace.*
>
> —Romans 11:6

FOR THE CREAM AND CRIMSON

Are you trying to work or buy your way into heaven? Do you think that if you are a good person then that's good enough to get a pass? Do you believe that if you stick to the Ten Commandments then God will give you a nod and allow you to enter the pearly gates? How about just showing up for the Christmas and Easter services at your church? Is that enough?

---

10 Pete DiPrimio, "Hoosiers Throttle Terrapins," Indiana University Athletics, November 1, 2025, https://iuhoosiers.com/news/2025/11/1/football-hoosiers-throttle-terrapins-PETE.

HOO-HOO-HOO-HOOSIERS!

Doing good works for the Lord is fantastic. But you do those things because you are a Christian and not to get on the free-pass list to heaven. There is a commitment that must take place and that involves giving your heart and soul to the Lord Jesus Christ. Just as the Hoosiers paid the price in the offseason, you, too, need to do the same thing. You must dedicate your life to the Master and King of kings. Salvation is the gift, and you cannot earn your way into heaven. There are some misconceptions out there from the devil concerning this issue. Here are some lies he may have tried to slip in your ear.

1. It's a family affair. Just because your great-great grandparents, great grandparents, grandparents, and parents were all Christians, doesn't mean you are covered. You cannot enter the kingdom on their coattails. Salvation is a deep and personal experience. If Satan tells you this, he is misleading you into darkness.

2. Works will do it for you. Satan will try to convince you that tossing some money in the offering plate and giving some money to charities will be enough to get you to heaven. He's a liar. First of all, tithing to your local church is a command and not up for discussion. You do good works because Christ lives in you and you want to do good to others. "In the same way, let your light shine before others, so that they may see your good works and give glory to your Father who is in heaven" (Matthew 5:16).

3. Just be a good person. The devil will say that as long as you don't break any of the big rules, you will be fine in the end. The devil does not want you to have a personal relationship with Christ. What he doesn't tell you is that having a personal relationship is the best thing ever.

4. Just take communion. If you show up on special occasions and participate in special services like communion, then God will not send you to the lake of fire. You are right—God will not condemn you to hell—you will. God has paid the price through His Son Jesus Christ for you to have eternal life. Remember, the devil is a liar. "And no wonder, for even Satan disguises himself as an angel of light" (2 Corinthians 11:14).

5. You don't have to live the life. The devil will try to convince you to just go up and tell everyone you are a Christian and that will be enough to get everyone off your back. Again, the devil is a liar. If you decide to follow Christ, then you will love and want to live the Christian life. It's a life of love, hope, and peace. "For God so loved the world, that he gave his only Son, that whoever believes in him should not perish but have eternal life" (John 3:16).

The Christian life cannot be earned. It's offered, and the only way to have it is to accept and live the life. If you've been told that you can earn your way into heaven, you've been lied to over the years. Make the decision to follow Christ, and the good works you do will be bonus points.

DAY 11

THERE'S NOT MUCH TIME LEFT

November 8, 2025: Indiana 27, Penn State 24

Therefore, stay awake, for you do not know on what day your Lord is coming.

—Matthew 24:42

With less than two minutes remaining in the game and no time-outs, the Indiana Hoosiers trailed 24–20.

A field goal would not help. They needed a touchdown to stay undefeated and to stay in the College Football Playoff discussion. After Indiana quarterback Fernando Mendoza was sacked, he orchestrated an eighty-yard drive in just ten plays. The game-winning drive culminated when he connected with Omar Cooper, who demonstrated his athletic agility with a toe-tapping catch in the back of the end zone, for the fourteen-yard TD.

On the final drive, Mendoza completed five of eight passes for the entire eighty yards. The Hoosiers showed poise, grace under fire, and a determination to win. Indiana stayed unbeaten at 10–0 and 7–0 in the Big Ten. The seventeen-point come-from-behind win by the Hoosiers was the first one ever at

Beaver Stadium. And they pulled it off without any time-outs left and as time ran out on the clock.

How much time do you have?

> *Therefore you also must be ready, for the Son of Man is coming at an hour you do not expect.*
>
> —Matthew 24:44

FOR THE CREAM AND CRIMSON

You will go through this life at breakneck speed. Before you know it, you will be in your twilight years. What have you done with your time? Did you spend it wisely? Foolishly? Will you make the most of what time you have remaining? Perhaps you are in the middle of life. What is more important to you right now? Maybe you are in the planning stages of your life. What is on your to-do list?

HOO-HOO-HOO-HOOSIERS!

Don't waste what time you have left in this world. It will be gone in a heartbeat. You, as a believer in Christ, are encouraged to do what you can to spread kindness along with the good news of Christ. Life is short, and time cannot be recovered or replaced. Make your investments meaningful and not wasted. Spend time with your family and friends and worshipping the Lord. Don't squander time on things in this world that don't hold value. Relationships matter. Here are some things to consider about time.

1. Know it's limited. You are given twenty-four hours in one day, and none of it is a guarantee. You don't know when time will cease for you. Make sure you are accountable for your time. Go to your kid's games. Visit that person in the hospital. Take vacations with your family. Don't spend it as much at the office. Time with God and your family is more precious than a three-car garage. You have to work to make a living, but make time for what matters.

2. Realize it has significance. What you do now for the kingdom is vital. What you do in sin also has consequences. You should focus your time on things of eternal significance. Does that mean you can't play golf or go fishing with your buddies? No. Relaxation is a must. But limit that time and prioritize it on things to help others. "But the one who endures to the end will be saved" (Matthew 24:13).

3. Use it with wisdom. You cannot get the time back that you may have wasted, but you can learn going forward. "Look carefully then how you walk, not as unwise but as wise, making the best use of the time, because the days are evil. Therefore do not be foolish, but understand what the will of the Lord is" (Ephesians 5:15–17).

4. Don't bank it; spend it. Procrastination is a bad habit. Do you know of anyone who put off taking a vacation or trip with their parents and regretted not taking it in time? What you put off today may not present itself tomorrow. That doesn't mean to go out and blow all

your money on things and put it on credit. It means that time is ticking, and you should do what matters the most with the people who matter the most. Don't have any regrets. If you are not a Christian at this time, don't rely on a deathbed conversion. They do happen, but why risk it? "But the day of the Lord will come like a thief, and then the heavens will pass away with a roar, and the heavenly bodies will be burned up and dissolved, and the earth and the works that are done on it will be exposed" (2 Peter 3:10).

5. Be intentional with time. Try to actively seek out opportunities to serve God and others and treat each day as a new chance to make a positive impact on the world around you. God has given you time. Time to play. Time to pray. Time to live. Time to work. "Whatever you do, work heartily, as for the Lord and not for men, knowing that from the Lord you will receive the inheritance as your reward. You are serving the Lord Christ" (Colossians 3:23–24).

Time is an irreplaceable gift from the Lord to you. He meant for you to accomplish eternal purposes with it and serve Him along the journey. Life is brief and the most valuable asset you will have. Spend it with love and don't take for granted that it will always be there, because it won't.

DAY 12

REFUSE TO LOSE

November 8, 2025: Indiana 27, Penn State 24

All Scripture is breathed out by God and profitable for teaching, for reproof, for correction, and for training in righteousness.

—2 Timothy 3:16

This is the second chapter inspired by Indiana's win over Penn State. On day 11, you read how the Hoosiers came from behind in the final two minutes to knock off Big Ten rival Penn State at Happy Valley—a notoriously difficult place for any college football team to play.

Indiana struggled throughout most of the game in all areas—offense, defense, and special teams. The defense gave up seventeen unanswered points in the second half, but they stayed focused on the task at hand. Although the Hoosiers did not dominate, they did put themselves in position to win in the end.

Indiana's defense stiffened when it needed to and was able to stop the Nittany Lions and force them to give the ball back to the Hoosiers. Quarterback Fernando Mendoza put together an eighty-yard drive in ten plays without any time-outs in the final two minutes to win the game.

Indiana coach Curt Cignetti said over and over in the postgame press conference that the team "refused to lose."[11] That was true, and the Hoosiers did enough to win when the pressure was on.

> *Behold, I stand at the door and knock. If anyone hears my voice and opens the door, I will come in to him and eat with him, and he with me.*
>
> —Revelation 3:20

FOR THE CREAM AND CRIMSON

In life's four quarters, there will be days when you can only do just enough. You won't have your A game all the time. There will be times when you struggle personally, mentally, and spiritually. There might be times when you are not up to the task at hand, but you have to put yourself in position to finish strong. Do you refuse to lose?

HOO-HOO-HOO-HOOSIERS!

You might be going through a struggle and just need to know someone cares. That He cares. Discouragement is real. Frustration is real. You can only put on a happy face so often, right? When life is out of your control, do you still put yourself in position to score on the last drive? This might sound basic and

11 Daniel Flick, "What Curt Cignetti Said After Indiana Football's Win over Penn State," *Sports Illustrated*, November 8, 2025, https://www.si.com/college/indiana/football/curt-cignetti-said-indiana-football-win-penn-state-transcript-mendoza-cooper.

simple, but here are some things to do when you are faced with an eighty-yard drive to win with no time-outs and with the clock ticking.

1. Just pray. Talk to the Lord. Pour your heart out. Give thanks and give Him praise because He is worthy, but let it out. Ask for a miracle. Ask for guidance. Ask for help. "Praying at all times in the Spirit, with all prayer and supplication. To that end, keep alert with all perseverance, making supplication for all the saints" (Ephesians 6:18).

2. Just read. Get into the Word of God. Don't do this out of desperation but as a daily objective to improve your relationship with the Lord. The Hoosier athletes know their playbook, and you should know yours as well. Read it. Get lost in it. Learn from the wisdom within the pages. "So faith comes from hearing, and hearing through the word of Christ" (Romans 10:17).

3. Just attend. Go to church on a regular basis. A football team cannot win a game if it doesn't show up to play. The church is your practice field and stadium for life. Show up. Praise Him. Be fed.

4. Just reach out. Meet your pastor over coffee and talk about what's going on in your life. Find a friend and talk with them in confidence. Sometimes you just need to vent. Don't look for or make excuses but talk about

solutions. "A friend loves at all times, / and a brother is born for adversity" (Proverbs 17:17).

5. Just wait. This is hard. It's a test of faith at times. Pray and talk to the Lord and read His Word and pray again. Worship Him at His house, and let your troubles out to your friends or a confidant. Then wait on His time. You might want that certain job so bad—wait. You might have an earthly desire to try to solve a problem that keeps getting bigger—wait. Trust His timing. You'll be glad when it's over.

When the entire season was on the line, the Hoosiers refused to lose. The mental part of the game is the hardest. This is true in life too. When the devil has you down, refuse to lose. Pick yourself up and trust the Lord. He will deliver you when you least expect it to happen.

DAY 13

GET SOME REST

November 15, 2025: Indiana 31, Wisconsin 7

Come to me, all who labor and are heavy laden, and I will give you rest. Take my yoke upon you, and learn from me, for I am gentle and lowly in heart, and you will find rest for your souls. For my yoke is easy, and my burden is light.

—Matthew 11:28–30

The No. 2 Hoosiers knocked off Wisconsin 31–7 at Merchants Bank Field at Memorial Stadium to start the season 11–0 for the first time in the university's history. The win also put Indiana at 8–0 in the Big Ten Conference.

Indiana quarterback Fernando Mendoza completed twenty-two of twenty-four passes (91 percent) for 299 yards with four touchdowns and, once again, no interceptions. After this victory, the Hoosiers had a bye week the next week, and Indiana head coach Curt Cignetti said it came at a fantastic time.

"It's our 11th win in a row, which is one more than last year," Cignetti said in an article posted on IUHoosiers.com. "It's great to enter an off week, get the players and assistant coaches some rest. We need some rest. A lot of guys are banged up. We want to get healed up as much as possible."[12]

> *Thus says the* Lord*:*
> *"Stand by the roads, and look,*
> *and ask for the ancient paths,*
> *where the good way is; and walk in it,*
> *and find rest for your souls."*
>
> —Jeremiah 6:16

FOR THE CREAM AND CRIMSON

Is your daily routine a blur? Do you find yourself having trouble keeping up with your schedule? Do you try to push your time with God in as quick as possible? Are you exhausted? This is exactly what the devil wants you to be. He wants you to neglect your spiritual obligations. He wants you to experience burnout. He wants you to forget about your kid's practice and games. He wants to distract you from attending church and family functions. He wants to defeat you.

HOO-HOO-HOO-HOOSIERS!

If you can juggle all your obligations, that's great. But if you are stressed out over life and what's going on in your surroundings, you need to do one thing: REST. A hectic lifestyle can put a

12 Pete DiPrimio, "Hoosiers Top Badgers on Senior Day," Indiana University Athletics, November 15, 2025, https://iuhoosiers.com/news/2025/11/15/football-hoosiers-sweep-home-slate-PETE.

strain on all your relationships, and if you're not careful, you will neglect those who are important to you. Here are some great reasons to REST.

1. Even God did this. On the seventh day, the Lord took a day off after He created the world in six days. You need to rest, period. This will help you avoid burnout and mistakes. Take a regular day off. Unwind when you get home. Put the phone away. "And on the seventh day God finished his work that he had done, and he rested on the seventh day from all his work that he had done. So God blessed the seventh day and made it holy, because on it God rested from all his work that he had done in creation" (Genesis 2:2–3).

2. It strengthens your faith. When you take a break and rest, then you have faith in God that He will provide. Don't rely on your effort; trust and show faith in Christ. "Let us therefore strive to enter that rest, so that no one may fall by the same sort of disobedience" (Hebrews 4:11).

3. It will restore your mental health. You are human and will tire out at some point in the day. When you unplug, you and everyone around you is better off in the long run. Your mental health is more important than any career. When you get rest, it helps you put your faith in perspective. "The LORD is my shepherd; I shall not want" (Psalm 23:1).

4. Rest will reenergize you. Your body and mind need time to heal. You can overwork your mind and body if you are not proactive. If you don't rest, you will eventually miss out in a big way.

5. Just get away. Throughout the New Testament, Jesus got away from everyone and rested. And what did He do? He invited the weary to follow His example and do the same. "Therefore, while the promise of entering his rest still stands, let us fear lest any of you should seem to have failed to reach it" (Hebrews 4:1).

Coach Cignetti knew the importance of rest. He knew his team and coaches needed to unwind for a few days. He was aware what was at stake: a perfect season, a shot at the Big Ten Championship, a berth in the playoffs, and a potential national championship. The goals were clear and the rest was needed. Get some rest.

DAY 14

ARE YOU A MISFIT?

November 28, 2025: Indiana 56, Purdue 3

Do not be conformed to this world, but be transformed by the renewal of your mind, that by testing you may discern what is the will of God, what is good and acceptable and perfect.

—Romans 12:2

The game was less a contest and more of a coronation. Indiana put a stamp on a perfect season with a 56–3 thumping of Purdue to end the regular season 12–0 and 9–0 in the Big Ten and secure a date with Ohio State for the conference championship at Lucas Oil Stadium in Indianapolis.

With the win over Purdue on the road, the Hoosiers claimed the Old Oaken Bucket trophy for a second straight time. Running back Roman Hemby blew through the Boilermaker defense for 156 yards on twelve carries with a TD while Kaelon Black rumbled sixty-seven yards on thirteen carries with two scores. Quarterback Fernando Mendoza had an average day and completed eight of fifteen passes for 117 yards and two touchdowns.

"This team is a bunch of misfits across the nation and now we are 12–0," Mendoza said in an article published on IUHoosiers.com. "It's a special group of guys." He went on to say that the team is unique and special. "All of us worked all of our lives to get to this point," he said in the article. "There's no complacency. We have to go harder, train harder. This is a once in a lifetime opportunity."[13]

Are you a misfit? Do you find problems fitting in where most people seem at ease?

> *For by the grace given to me I say to everyone among you not to think of himself more highly than he ought to think, but to think with sober judgment, each according to the measure of faith that God has assigned.*
>
> —Romans 12:3

FOR THE CREAM AND CRIMSON

You are unique and special in the eyes of the Lord. But do you feel out of place in society? How about in church? Do you have a place and fit in? If you don't, it's OK. You can find your belonging by shifting your focus from conforming to a certain "religious" mold to embracing who you are in Christ.

---

13 Pete DiPrimio, "Bucket Stays in Bloomington," Indiana University Athletics, November 28, 2025, https://iuhoosiers.com/news/2025/11/28/football-bucket-stays-in-bloomington-PETE.

HOO-HOO-HOO-HOOSIERS!

Sometimes you have to escape the judgment and find peace and acceptance elsewhere. You can find your God-given place and role within the body of Christ. You must not rebel, but at the same time, embrace your gifts. Churches have rules and if you are not comfortable with them, examine yourself or find another place of worship. You must respect the leadership and rules and not be a person of confrontation. Here are some ways you can fit in and find your place in a misfit world.

1. Embrace your uniqueness. You are unique, but your circumstance is not. Moses had a problem with speech and some of the disciples were misfits. And don't forget about King David. He was a shepherd boy (a misfit) who later became a king and who chased God's heart. Never compare yourself, but instead embrace who you are in Christ. "I praise you, for I am fearfully and wonderfully made. / Wonderful are your works; / my soul knows it very well" (Psalm 139:14).

2. Get involved. Work with organizations that get down to the nitty-gritty. Volunteer with food banks or food pantries and feed the hungry. Connect with people and help others in the field. Consider a mission trip or even becoming a missionary. You might be that special person God is calling.

3. Find your community. Look for small groups or social groups with people who share your unique

characteristics. They are out there. If you don't fit in where you are, find where you do. Be patient and connect. God will open the door. "Ask, and it will be given to you; seek, and you will find; knock, and it will be opened to you" (Matthew 7:7).

4. Always focus on Christ. You are a child of the King. He has invited you to "come and dine." Don't let others take away your reservation. Focus on the love of Jesus in your heart and keep true to your faith. It's yours and no one can take that away. "Seek the LORD and his strength; / seek his presence continually!" (Psalm 105:4).

5. Recognize your church. Find a church that welcomes you and does not judge you. A true church is made up of a diverse group of misfits who have accepted Christ as their Savior. If everyone was the same, it would be a boring church. You are special. You are loved. You are needed in a church community. You are enough.

The Hoosiers, as Mendoza said, were a bunch of misfits who worked together for one mission: to win. The ultimate goal as a believer is for you to fit in and force change where you are. Find your place. It's there. God is there.

DAY 15

BE CONSISTENT—NOT PERFECT!

November 28, 2025: Indiana 56, Purdue 3

Jesus Christ is the same yesterday and today and forever.
—Hebrews 13:8

Going undefeated in the regular season deserves a second chapter. The game itself was a bold statement—the Hoosiers are for real.

Hoosier running back Kaelon Black had two touchdowns on the ground, and quarterback Fernando Mendoza and Roman Hemby each ran for another as the No. 2 Indiana Hoosiers thumped Big Ten rival Purdue 56–3 on Friday night, completing the first perfect regular season in school history and securing a Big Ten Championship game berth.

The moment was unreal. It was long overdue.

Indiana celebrated by hoisting the Old Oaken Bucket in the series' one hundredth trophy game, while head coach Curt Cignetti became the first Hoosiers coach since Bo McMillin in 1934–35 to win his first two matchups against Purdue.

"Week after week, they've just been consistent, very coachable, done what we've asked them to do," Cignetti said in an article published by WDRB. "They've stacked meetings, days, practices, showed up, prepared, put it between the white lines, and pretty darn consistent in all three phases. Got a bunch of great, high-character guys on this team, and I give the coaches a ton of credit."[14]

Week after week, Cignetti often told reporters that the team still needed to improve in certain areas. Players also echoed those words and knew that perfection on the field is almost impossible—but they could be consistent.

It worked. They achieved a perfect regular season by consistency. How consistent are you in your daily walk with Christ?

> *Because you did not serve the Lord your God with joyfulness and gladness of heart, because of the abundance of all things, therefore you shall serve your enemies whom the Lord will send against you, in hunger and thirst, in nakedness, and lacking everything. And he will put a yoke of iron on your neck until he has destroyed you.*
>
> —Deuteronomy 28:47–48

FOR THE CREAM AND CRIMSON

No one expects you to be perfect, except maybe you. But deep down you know that's an impossible task. But you try. In some areas you succeed in your quest, but more times than not, you

14 Eric Crawford, "Undefeated! Indiana Finishes Perfect Regular Season with 56–3 Win at Purdue," WDRB, November 28, 2025, https://www.wdrb.com/sports/crawford-undefeated-indiana-finishes-perfect-regular-season-with-56-3-win-at-purdue/article_6cc7d71e-3deb-4bf5-8d2e-8c3708f6e23c.html.

probably fail. It's OK. High expectations are great to have. It gives you something to shoot for.

HOO-HOO-HOO-HOOSIERS!

You've heard the old saying that being perfect is boring. It's also unattainable. Only Christ fit that mold. But you can do what Coach Cignetti and the Hoosiers strived for and that was consistency. It worked out for them. You can build consistency by setting spiritual habits and sticking to a routine. With this, you can establish a solid faith and something you can count on when times become tough. And being consistent is not hard at all. It's just doing the little things on a regular basis. Here are some ways you can be consistent in your daily walk.

1. Set a time devoted for you and God. Establish a quiet time where you and the Lord can visit. The Hoosiers and all teams have set times when they work out and get their bodies in shape for competition. You need to do the same. Whether it's in the morning or evening, set a time and don't allow distractions to interfere. "But when you pray, go into your room and shut the door and pray to your Father who is in secret. And your Father who sees in secret will reward you" (Matthew 6:6).

2. Do the little things. Don't bite off too much at once. Consistency beats intensity. Start out by reading one chapter of your Bible a day as a suggestion and study what God tells you. Do the same in your prayer life. Keep it simple, but do it on a consistent basis. As time grows, so will your desire.

3. Give yourself some grace. If you miss a time or day, it's OK. Don't beat yourself up or give up. Make a note of where you stopped and also try to make up for the missed day. Keep going. Mendoza missed some pass attempts but kept going. "For sin will have no dominion over you, since you are not under law but under grace" (Romans 6:14).

4. Start a community support group. A team relies on each other, and you need the same. Organize a small group of friends or like-minded people to meet on a regular basis and help one another. There is nothing like support and accountability. "And let us consider how to stir up one another to love and good works, not neglecting to meet together, as is the habit of some, but encouraging one another, and all the more as you see the Day drawing near" (Hebrews 10:24–25).

5. Journal. This isn't for everybody, but you might find it helpful. Invest in a nice journal and write down what you hope to accomplish each day or what happened or a prayer list. Go back and review often to see how God has worked in your life and answered prayers.

You cannot reach perfection as a human, but you can be consistent. The Hoosiers went undefeated in the regular season but had moments when they gave up touchdowns to the other team and even had to come back a couple of times to win. You can do the same. Be consistent in your daily walk and do the little things, and you will be victorious.

DAY 16

STICK TOGETHER

December 6, 2025: Indiana 13, Ohio State 10

Big Ten Championship

Let all bitterness and wrath and anger and clamor and slander be put away from you, along with all malice. Be kind to one another, tenderhearted, forgiving one another, as God in Christ forgave you.

—Ephesians 4:31–32

It happened. The Indiana Hoosiers knocked off No. 1 Ohio State to win the Big Ten Championship and take a huge step in their overall quest to claim a national title. The game was an offensive struggle for both teams, but Indiana quarterback Fernando Mendoza's 17-yard TD pass to Elijah Sarratt was all the Hoosiers needed to take the crown away from the Buckeyes.

The win kept Indiana's streak at 13–0 and snapped a thirty-game losing streak to Ohio State. It was the first time the Hoosiers football team would reach the No. 1 spot after dethroning Ohio State, who had beaten Indiana sixteen straight times.

"'We were never supposed to be in this position, but now we're the flipping champs,' Mendoza shouted on television before he was selected the game's MVP. 'We are brothers, we know how to stick together and we're the toughest glue ever.'"[15]

Do you help a brother or sister in need?

> *But if anyone has the world's goods and sees his brother in need, yet closes his heart against him, how does God's love abide in him?*
>
> —1 John 3:17

FOR THE CREAM AND CRIMSON

Have you ever been in a situation where you did not want to be nice? Perhaps you've been assigned a task at work with some people whom you don't get along with. Or maybe you were cut off in traffic and finally pull up next to the person who made you slam on your brakes. Are you friendly? Do you stick together? Are you the type of person who will help out a friend or carry someone's burden with them? Are you understanding and patient?

HOO-HOO-HOO-HOOSIERS!

You can strengthen your attitude and unity toward your fellow brother or sister and practice biblical love. There are moments when it may be a challenge, but you can meet and overcome those challenges, just like the Hoosiers did when they overcame the Buckeyes. Instead of fostering hostility and frustration at

---

15 Associated Press, "Indiana Downs Ohio State, 13–10, in the Discover Big Ten Football Championship Game," Big Ten, December 6, 2025, https://bigten.org/fb/article/59055/.

times, you can lift up your friends and bear a burden with them. You may not have any idea what they are going through, but you can be there for them and let them see your faith in action. Here are some great ways you can stick together and help out a friend.

1. Be intentional. Pray for one another and do life together. You will find that when you give more encouragement than criticism, you will become stronger in your faith, and your attitude will improve.

2. Have a service-minded attitude. Become involved in local charities or civic organizations and be a part of a solution. There are many groups out there that do great things; be a part of one of them. "For you were called to freedom, brothers. Only do not use your freedom as an opportunity for the flesh, but through love serve one another" (Galatians 5:13).

3. Forgive and unify. When you bear a burden with a friend instead of talking about them behind their back, you practice humility and compassion. Do something that is a challenge and help them. Let others criticize if they want. "Anyone whom you forgive, I also forgive. Indeed, what I have forgiven, if I have forgiven anything, has been for your sake in the presence of Christ" (2 Corinthians 2:10).

4. Build a relationship. When you tell someone that you will pray for them, actually do it right there. Chitchat and words are one thing, but action speaks louder.

Listen to them and let them know they are not forgotten. "Love one another with brotherly affection. Outdo one another in showing honor" (Romans 12:10).

5. Take advantage of technology. If you cannot be there in a physical sense, then use technology to reach them. Use social media and apps to help connect with some who are lonely.

Stick together and be a person who can be depended on for help. Do your role and stay in your lane and be someone others can be inspired by. Mendoza and the Hoosiers stuck together and did the impossible with teamwork and determination. Never think you are bigger than the moment, and be the one who encourages.

DAY 17

GIVE THE GLORY TO GOD IN ALL THINGS

December 6, 2025: Indiana 13, Ohio State 10

Big Ten Championship

Thus says the Lord*: "Let not the wise man boast in his wisdom, let not the mighty man boast in his might, let not the rich man boast in his riches, but let him who boasts boast in this, that he understands and knows me, that I am the* Lord *who practices steadfast love, justice, and righteousness in the earth. For in these things I delight, declares the* Lord*."*

—Jeremiah 9:23–24

A win is a win and the Hoosiers will take it any way they can earn it.

Such was the case on December 6 when Indiana hung on to win the Big Ten Conference Championship 13–10 after Ohio State placekicker Jayden Fielding missed a twenty-seven-yard field goal in the final minutes. The field goal would have tied the game and may have changed the overall outcome. But it wasn't meant to be. The Hoosiers won the game and continued their quest toward a national championship.

The victory was Indiana's first outright conference championship since 1945, after a shared win in 1967. Going into the game, the Hoosiers were four-point underdogs against the defending national champions and the No. 1-ranked team in the nation. On the line was a top seed in the College Football Playoffs.

Indiana quarterback Fernando Mendoza was brilliant despite getting injured on the game's first play. He completed fifteen of twenty-three passes for 222 yards and tossed one touchdown and had one intercepted.

"I want to give all the glory to God," Mendoza said on Fox Sports on the field after the win. "We were never supposed to be in this position, but by the glory of God, the great coaches, the great teammates, everybody around us, we were able to pull this off."[16]

> *And every tongue confess that Jesus Christ is Lord, to the glory of God the Father.*
>
> —Philippians 2:11

16 Jackson Thompson, "Indiana Wins First Outright Big 10 Football Title Since 1945 After Ohio State Flubs Short Field Goal Try," Fox News, December 6, 2025, https://www.foxnews.com/sports/indiana-wins-first-outright-big-10-football-championship-since-1945-after-ohio-state-flubs-short-field-goal.

FOR THE CREAM AND CRIMSON

Do you let little things slip by without giving God the glory He deserves? The Lord is the Master of the universe and warrants praise from His creation. You probably thank Him for the big events and happenings in your life, as you should. You will glorify Him for that big job you landed or for healing or for your safety when you travel. But what about the smaller happenings? What about things you don't know about?

HOO-HOO-HOO-HOOSIERS!

Do you give honor and glory to God for taking you a different way to work, and then you find out later there was an accident on your usual way? What about keeping your children or grandchildren safe at day care? You are called to give God glory because it's your fundamental purpose in existing. You are to acknowledge Him and recognize His holiness in your life. Do you do this? Are you afraid you will be labeled if you give Him credit like Mendoza did on national television? Here are some reasons why you should give God glory in all things.

1. He deserves praise. He is the ruler of the universe and is the reason you are here in the first place. Did you recognize the Hoosiers as the Big Ten Conference champs after they beat Ohio State? Of course you did because they earned it. God has earned your praise. "With my mouth I will give great thanks to the LORD; / I will praise him in the midst of the throng" (Psalm 109:30).

2. It keeps you humble. By giving God glory, it will help you turn attention away from selfish ambitions and allow you to live life with more joy and happiness. It's OK to be successful, but make sure you attribute your success to Him because He gave it to you and can take it away.

3. You acknowledge His power. It's not about you; it's about Him. This is an easy one to get lost in because you are human. Everything you do, and don't do, is because that is how He wants it for you. You might think you are in control, but you are not. "O LORD, you are my God; / I will exalt you; I will praise your name, / for you have done wonderful things, / plans formed of old, faithful and sure" (Isaiah 25:1).

4. You witness to others. Live a life that reflects God's character and makes the Christian life look fun to your friends and family. When Mendoza told the world that he thanked God, he was having fun. Do life with a smile.

5. Praise lifts your overall attitude. When you lift your hands and voice in praise, it's hard not to be in a good mood. You may be facing struggles and battles, but you can go through them with the Lord on your side. "Blessed be the God and Father of our Lord Jesus Christ! According to his great mercy, he has caused us to be born again to a living hope through the resurrection of Jesus Christ from the dead" (1 Peter 1:3).

When Indiana won the Big Ten Conference Championship, Hoosier Nation was exuberant. They laughed and cried and celebrated because they had just captured the title. You as a Christian should be in a similar attitude in your daily walk. You know the outcome in life. Be happy and praise Him in all things.

DAY 18

WHAT'S YOUR GOLIATH?

December 6, 2025: Indiana 13, Ohio State 10

Big Ten Championship

Then he took his staff in his hand and chose five smooth stones from the brook and put them in his shepherd's pouch. His sling was in his hand, and he approached the Philistine.

—1 Samuel 17:40

Although Indiana entered the Big Ten Championship game ranked No. 2, they were still heavy underdogs against No. 1 Ohio State. The Buckeyes, all the prognosticators said, were destined to repeat as National Champions, and Indiana was a mere speed bump. But the Hoosiers had other ideas.

The game was a defensive battle, but IU held to its game plan and stunned the Buckeyes and the college football world with a 13–10 upset win.

"We're going to go in the playoffs as the No. 1 seed, and a lot of people probably thought that wasn't possible," Indiana head coach Curt Cignetti said in an article published by Indiana

Daily Student. "But when you get the right people and you have a plan and they love one another and play for one another and they commit, anything's possible. And I think that's what you saw happen here."[17]

The Hoosiers outgained OSU 340–322 in total yards and outrushed them on the ground with 118 yards to fifty-eight. But Indiana wide receiver Charlie Becker had a tremendous game and caught six passes for twenty-six yards. In the article, Becker said the moment was "surreal," as he grew up cheering for OSU.

In the end, Indiana pulled off a stunning shocker of an upset and sent the mighty Buckeyes home for the rest of the season.

What is your Goliath?

> *Then David said to the Philistine, "You come to me with a sword and with a spear and with a javelin, but I come to you in the name of the* Lord *of hosts, the God of the armies of Israel, whom you have defied."*
>
> —1 Samuel 17:45

FOR THE CREAM AND CRIMSON

You will face battles along your Christian journey, and some may be too big to overcome in your mind. You may experience fear, anxiety, and worry over issues out of your control. Perhaps your Goliath is greed and materialism. Maybe you battle addiction. Perhaps your struggle is with immorality and compromising your

17 Dalton James, "Flippin' Champs," *Indiana Daily Student*, December 8, 2025, https://issuu.com/idsnews/docs/indiana_daily_student_-_monday_dec._8_2025.

beliefs when no one is around. Maybe your Goliath is pride. The devil also uses depression and discouragement through disappointing circumstances.

HOO-HOO-HOO-HOOSIERS!

Goliaths come into your life to strengthen you, but you must be aware of those moments. You can defeat your Goliath whether it's a broken relationship or financial hardships, workplace pressures or health issues. The overall thought is that you cannot overcome your Goliath alone. In fact, you must trust in the Lord to have any chance of victory. Here are some ways you can thrust the stone at your Goliath.

1. Have complete trust in His power. When David defeated Goliath, it proved that the Lord can do anything. But you must be the one with faith and trust. "Commit your way to the LORD; / trust in him, and he will act" (Psalm 37:5).

2. Focus on the Lord and not the size of your Goliath. Your problem might be mammoth in size and daunting. But God is bigger. Remember that.

3. Use scripture to inspire. Put to memory some scripture verse that helps encourage you in times of pressure. "For I know the plans I have for you, declares the LORD, plans for welfare and not for evil, to give you a future and a hope" (Jeremiah 29:11).

4. Recall the past. Think back to times when God delivered you from some of your problems. This will give you encouragement to keep going.

5. Expect and act in faith. The Hoosiers did not back down. Instead, they entered the stadium and expected to win. They faced challenges during the game but relied on one another. Confide in a friend or a pastor and hit the field. "Do your best to present yourself to God as one approved, a worker who has no need to be ashamed, rightly handling the word of truth" (2 Timothy 2:15).

Victory over the Buckeyes did not just happen. It was achieved through hard work and determination. Life is not easy. Be prepared to fight battles but make sure you put the Lord under center to lead you to victory. God is bigger than any Goliath.

DAY 19

LEAVE NO DOUBT

January 1, 2026: Indiana 38, Alabama 3

CFP Quarterfinals

For God so loved the world, that he gave his only Son, that whoever believes in him should not perish but have eternal life.

—John 3:16

CBS Sports described it best: "Indiana Throttles Alabama: Hoosiers Leave No Doubt En Route to CFP Semifinal Berth Against Oregon." That was the headline and it stated the truth.

The No. 1 Hoosiers dismantled Alabama and, according to Cameron Salerno's article, "made a statement" as they rolled over the Tide.[18] Indiana head coach Curt Cignetti made college football history as the second FBS coach to win at least

18 Cameron Salerno, "Indiana Throttles Alabama: Hoosiers Leave No Doubt En Route to CFP Semifinal Berth Against Oregon," CBS Sports, January 1, 2026, https://www.cbssports.com/college-football/news/alabama-indiana-live-updates-rose-bowl-score-result-analysis-college-football-playoff/live/.

twenty-five games in his first two seasons at the university. Hoosier quarterback Fernando Mendoza, fresh off winning the Heisman Trophy, had a fantastic day and completed fourteen of sixteen passes (87 percent) for 192 yards and three touchdowns.

The defeat was Alabama's worst since 2000, but the Hoosier win sent a message to the whole world that Indiana was for real. They left no doubt in anyone's mind that they belonged.

What message do you send? Are you for real?

> *I have been crucified with Christ. It is no longer I who live, but Christ who lives in me. And the life I now live in the flesh I live by faith in the Son of God, who loved me and gave himself for me.*
>
> —Galatians 2:20

FOR THE CREAM AND CRIMSON

You might have a wonderful image as a Christian and attend church and do all the right things. That's fantastic. But do you really have the faith you need to make it to the championship game? Do you have any doubts? It's a serious question. Do you know some Christians who don't have a foolproof, locked-down testimony? Is there anything in your life that holds you back?

HOO-HOO-HOO-HOOSIERS!

Subtle doubts can creep into your mind, and that is how the devil operates. He does it in small doses. He wants you to eventually doubt your salvation. Is he successful with you? Here are some ways you can know without a shadow of a doubt that you will claim the prize at the end of the game.

1. Trust the promise. The Lord made you some promises, and you can take them to the bank. God promised unconditional love as well as meeting all your needs. He promised you peace and forgiveness if asked. He also promised to never leave or forsake you, and He promised a home in heaven if you are faithful. "It is better to take refuge in the LORD / than to trust in man" (Psalm 118:8).

2. Be obedient in all you do. Have a consistent walk with your heavenly Father and be quick to confess your sins and seek forgiveness. Make the effort to do better every day and correct your mistakes. Allow His love and mercy to work in your life every day. "But be doers of the word, and not hearers only, deceiving yourselves" (James 1:22).

3. Be unyielding in your devotion time. Put aside time every day to devote to Him and His Word and prayer. If you begin to slack, that's what the devil wants. If something interferes with your alone time, consider an alternative time slot. When you spend time with Him and the Word, you will become stronger in your faith. "Therefore, preparing your minds for action, and being sober-minded, set your hope fully on the grace that will be brought to you at the revelation of Jesus Christ" (1 Peter 1:13).

4. Focus on what *He* did for you. Don't focus on the negatives in your life but rather what He did you for. He died on a cross and rose from the grave and has prepared a place for you. He tossed your sins in the sea of forgetfulness and gave you a second, third, and fourth chance.

5. Hold to your convictions. Don't let weaker people in your life encourage you to do things you know are wrong just to fit in. Be a person of courage and valor. If you have any doubts, don't go through with it. "You believe that God is one; you do well. Even the demons believe—and shudder!" (James 2:19).

You can leave no doubt that your salvation is real and anchored in Christ. Assurance comes from trusting in the Word of God and through prayer. Just like the Hoosiers left no doubt they were for real, you can leave no doubt that your plans are to make it to heaven.

DAY 20

STAY ON THE HIGH OF GOD'S BLESSINGS

January 1, 2026: Indiana 38, Alabama 3

CFP Quarterfinals

And the peace of God, which surpasses all understanding, will guard your hearts and your minds in Christ Jesus.

—Philippians 4:7

A couple of weeks had passed since Indiana quarterback Fernando Mendoza won the prestigious Heisman Trophy, becoming the first Hoosier to be honored with the award.

Some football "experts" noted that Mendoza needed to avoid the next phase in the Heisman journey. The "Heisman jinx" is a widely discussed mythic hypothesis that suggests that winning the trophy leads to a lousy performance in the next bowl game. Some attribute it to extreme media pressure and the hangover effect from the high of winning.

Notable players who suffered from this were quarterbacks Jason White in 2003 and Bryce Young in 2021. Both won the

Heisman Trophy and then turned around and lost their next game.

Not Mendoza.

He led the No. 1 Hoosiers to a 38–3 thumping of No. 9 Alabama to advance to the CFP semifinal round against Oregon. In an article in TheDailyHoosier.com, Indiana head coach Curt Cignetti asked his QB to stay within himself and try not to be Superman after winning the award.[19]

Mendoza was efficient and accurate in the game and completed fourteen of sixteen passes with 192 yards and three TDs. He spread the ball around and connected with six different receivers and also ran for thirty-eight yards. He stayed grounded and kept his cool and avoided the "Heisman jinx." His attitude was not inflated by winning a major award. Instead, he stayed humble and played within his potential to guide the Hoosiers to the win.

Blessed is the man who trusts in the L*ORD*,
whose trust is the L*ORD*.
He is like a tree planted by water,
that sends out its roots by the stream,
and does not fear when heat comes,
for its leaves remain green,
and is not anxious in the year of drought,
for it does not cease to bear fruit.

—Jeremiah 17:7–8

19 Mike Schumann, "Curt Cignetti Called Fernando Mendoza to His Office When He Heard He Was Seeking Heisman Advice," *The Daily Hoosier*, October 31, 2025, https://www.thedailyhoosier.com/curt-cignetti-called-fernando-mendoza-to-his-office-when-he-heard-he-was-seeking-heisman-advice/.

FOR THE CREAM AND CRIMSON

How's your attitude? Do you find yourself taking credit for accomplishments? It's easy to get lost in conversations and bring the topic back to you. Do you dominate conversations? How is your tone? Is it condescending, and do you brag a lot? Do you dismiss others and their feelings? If you do, you may not intend to. But does it happen? Do you always have to top others' stories?

HOO-HOO-HOO-HOOSIERS!

Staying grounded and being humble can be hard to do at times, especially if you have a competitive nature. There is nothing wrong with recognition and winning awards. But how do you respond to the notoriety? Maybe you've been put in a position of authority at work or at your church. Here are some ways to stay grounded and avoid the "Heisman jinx."

1. Admit your mistakes. Recognize when you are wrong and apologize. There is nothing wrong with this. Don't make excuses and blame someone else. Own it. "For this very reason, make every effort to supplement your faith with virtue, and virtue with knowledge" (2 Peter 1:5).

2. Toss away the need to be recognized. Don't rely on praise from others, but accept it with grace when it happens. If God sees you, then that is all that matters.

3. Ask God for humility. Pride is a bad characteristic and can drive people away. Ask the Lord to show you areas where you show pride and to help you contain it (unless

you are a grandparent; then it's OK). "The reward for humility and fear of the LORD / is riches and honor and life" (Proverbs 22:4).

4. Listen to criticism. Don't become defensive when someone offers you a different perspective of yourself. There is a difference in constructive criticism and finding your faults. Listen and apply what you hear. "Know this, my beloved brothers: let every person be quick to hear, slow to speak, slow to anger; for the anger of man does not produce the righteousness of God" (James 1:19–20).

5. Don't take yourself too seriously. Laugh at yourself and see the humor in some of the things you do. Stay grounded and real to everyone. "He will yet fill your mouth with laughter, / and your lips with shouting" (Job 8:21).

Life is meant to be enjoyed. All of it. Don't get in the way and become the focus of attention. Mendoza knew his role. He was honored with the highest award in college football and did not let it go to his head. He kept his head and played well for his team. You can do the same. Take the awards you earn, show humility, and come through for your team when it counts.

DAY 21

GET OUT IN FRONT OF SIN

January 9, 2026: Indiana 56, Oregon 22

CFP Semifinals

Brothers, if anyone is caught in any transgression, you who are spiritual should restore him in a spirit of gentleness. Keep watch on yourself, lest you too be tempted.

—Galatians 6:1

Like a punch in the mouth, Indiana let Oregon know on the game's first play that they were going to win the contest.

Hoosier defensive back D'Angelo Ponds jumped a route and picked off Oregon quarterback Dante Moore's pass and scampered twenty-five yards into the end zone to send the message loud and clear. Soon after, IU junior quarterback Fernando Mendoza found Elijah Sarratt for a twenty-three-yard pass into Oregon territory.

Senior running back Roman Hemby rumbled twelve yards and ten yards before Mendoza connected with Omar Cooper for an eight-yard TD strike and the rout was on. Mendoza fired another TD, this time to sophomore wide receiver Charlie

Becker, who leaped and grabbed a thirty-six-yard pass in the end zone for the score.

The tone was set early in the game when Ponds recognized the pass and made good on the pick-six.

Do you recognize sin and temptations?

> *Preach the word; be ready in season and out of season; reprove, rebuke, and exhort, with complete patience and teaching.*
>
> —2 Timothy 4:2

FOR THE CREAM AND CRIMSON

The devil can disguise sin and make it appear to be fun and harmless. But the consequences of sin can be destructive. If it goes unchecked and unforgiven, the ramifications can linger for years. The primary consequence of sin is separation from God and can be deadly. You may experience broken relationships, guilt, and shame. The devil might pour it on and send you into depression and hopelessness. You could lose everything you have, including your health or job.

HOO-HOO-HOO-HOOSIERS!

Do you recognize the sin before it creates a path of destruction? What about a friend? Will you help a friend who may be going down the wrong path? Do you get involved and help or do you sit back and watch the train wreck? One of life's golden rules is to mind your own business. But is that what you are about?

Will you be the one who jumps the route? Here are some ways you can step in and help a friend or family member pick off the devil's plan of destruction.

1. Act and approach in love and humility. If you see a brother or sister struggling, be proactive and initiate a conversation. Make sure this is in private and pulled off with a spirit of kindness and not judgment. You are not above sin, so don't have an arrogant attitude. "But by the grace of God I am what I am, and his grace toward me was not in vain. On the contrary, I worked harder than any of them, though it was not I, but the grace of God that is with me" (1 Corinthians 15:10).

2. Don't downplay and accept the behavior. Love the sinner and not the sin. Let them know they are on a path that will not have a pleasant ending. Call them out in love and compassion.

3. Listen and understand. This is vital and often a lost art. Listen to them. Understand where your friend is coming from. Don't take the side of sin, but try to see their side of the story. When you listen, you validate the person and not their actions. "And have mercy on those who doubt; save others by snatching them out of the fire; to others show mercy with fear, hating even the garment stained by the flesh" (Jude 22–23).

4. Be of support. Encourage them to seek forgiveness and restitution. Let them know there is a way out. Offer to

walk through the storm with them, but let them know that you cannot take responsibility. "And though a man might prevail against one who is alone, two will withstand him—a threefold cord is not quickly broken" (Ecclesiastes 4:12).

5. Pray for them and with them. This can be huge. When you take time to pray with them, that will lift their spirits. Don't just say you'll pray for them, but actually do it. Make it a priority to do this in person and in private. Lift them up. "You also must help us by prayer, so that many will give thanks on our behalf for the blessing granted us through the prayers of many" (2 Corinthians 1:11).

Ponds made an impact on the game's first play and didn't wait for the fight to come to him. He made the statement and jumped the route. You can do the same for your friends and family by recognizing the devil's game play of destruction.

DAY 22

PROVE THEM ALL WRONG

January 9, 2026: Indiana 56, Oregon 22

CFP Semifinals

I am the vine; you are the branches. Whoever abides in me and I in him, he it is that bears much fruit, for apart from me you can do nothing.

—John 15:5

There wasn't much to say after Indiana walloped Oregon 56–22 in the Peach Bowl and advanced to the finals of the CFP Playoffs. The Hoosiers were on a mission, and it was the norm for them to soundly defeat their opponents on national television.

The No. 1-ranked Hoosiers blasted No. 5 Oregon and kept their doubters shaking their heads in disbelief. Indiana fired on all cylinders. The defense dominated. Special teams were effective and the offense was smooth and productive.

Indiana quarterback Fernando Mendoza was surgical. He connected on seventeen of twenty passes for 177 yards and five TDs. In just two CFP games, he completed thirty-one of thirty-six passes for 396 yards with eight touchdowns. His accuracy and decision-making were that of a veteran signal-caller. It was safe to say that Mendoza proved all the naysayers wrong who doubted that he should have won the Heisman Trophy.

Do you have doubters to prove wrong?

I can do all things through him who strengthens me.
—Philippians 4:13

FOR THE CREAM AND CRIMSON

After you made the decision to follow Christ in faith, were there people in your life who doubted your conversion? Did they just think you were being emotional and not serious about life? Perhaps they admired you at first, but then thought you'd go back to your old ways in a few days. Did they question you or try to "talk some sense" into you? Did they doubt that God changed you?

HOO-HOO-HOO-HOOSIERS!

You can, according to Barney Fife (Don Knotts), "nip this in the bud" right off the bat. You can address doubters by embodying the love of Jesus in your demeanor. You can demonstrate unwavering consistency and allow your transformation and salvation to be on full display for them to see. You don't need to put on an act. Don't argue, because that will give your doubters ammunition to antagonize you and reinforce their cause. Live out your faith. You will make mistakes along the way, but here are some tips to help prove your doubters wrong. And just maybe your influence will lead them to make the same decision for Christ that you made.

1. Be real. Allow your actions to do your talking. That's what Mendoza did. Be consistent in your character and let that serve as your public witness. Let them see a change. "For by grace you have been saved through faith. And this is not your own doing; it is the gift of God, not a result of works, so that no one may boast" (Ephesians 2:8–9).

2. Show love and patience. Stay away from judging others. (That never works.) Show kindness and love to your doubters. Don't accept bullying, but allow them to observe how kind and loving you can be toward them. "With all humility and gentleness, with patience, bearing with one another in love" (Ephesians 4:2).

3. Don't apologize. Know what you speak about before you engage in a conversation. Never apologize for following Christ. Be confident in your faith.

4. Don't argue. It's OK to have a discussion about your experience with Christ. If they doubt your experience, just let them see the happiness and joy and peace you have in life. Actions speak louder than words. "Do all things without grumbling or disputing" (Philippians 2:14).

5. Grow. This takes time. Stay in the Word of God, pray daily, and attend a church on a regular basis. You will grow, and your doubters will take note. "Practice these things, immerse yourself in them, so that all may see your progress" (1 Timothy 4:15).

Just be who God made you to be. In life, you will have those who support you and those who doubt you. That's just the way it is. But don't allow your doubters to dampen your experience. In the end, it doesn't matter what they think or do. Just do your best to show Christ every day and you'll find yourself in the championship game the next week.

DAY 23

YOU ARE ENOUGH

January 19, 2026: Indiana 27, Miami 21

CFP National Championship

Not that we are sufficient in ourselves to claim anything as coming from us, but our sufficiency is from God.
—2 Corinthians 3:5

For the first time in the history of Indiana University football, they had earned the title of National Champion. The No. 1-ranked Hoosiers hung on and knocked off Miami 27–21 to claim the College Football Playoff National Championship at Hard Rock Stadium in Miami Gardens, Florida.

Indiana football had won only thirteen bowl games in more than 130 years. But in two years, head coach Curt Cignetti turned the program around and went on a historic run to go 16–0 in the 2025–26 season.

Hoosier quarterback Fernando Mendoza threw for 186 yards on the night, but it was his twelve-yard scamper/dive into the end zone on fourth down in the fourth quarter that gave Indiana a ten-point lead.

The Hurricanes had a chance to tie the game, but quarterback Carson Beck's pass was picked off with forty-four seconds left in the game to secure the Indiana win. Mendoza told *60 Minutes* that the team was not predicted by experts to go this far.

"I was a two-star recruit," he said. "I wasn't a five star who's supposed to be in this position, who's supposed to be on the No. 1 team in the nation."[20] The Heisman Trophy winner basically said that many teams and universities passed on him and didn't think his ability was enough for their programs.

Have you ever felt you were not enough?

> *And God is able to make all grace abound to you, so that having all sufficiency in all things at all times, you may abound in every good work.*
>
> —2 Corinthians 9:8

FOR THE CREAM AND CRIMSON

Do you feel unwanted or unnoticed at times? Have you ever been rejected or experienced loneliness? Have you ever suffered from such low self-esteem or felt so bad about yourself that you slid away from society? Have you ever felt underappreciated, causing you to go to a dark place? You are not alone. You may feel isolated even in a crowd or in a congregation at church.

---

20 Jon Wertheim et al., "Indiana University Quarterback Fernando Mendoza, Head Coach Curt Cignetti on What's Behind Their Winning Streak," CBS News, December 14, 2025, https://www.cbsnews.com/news/indiana-university-football-cignetti-mendoza-60-minutes/.

HOO-HOO-HOO-HOOSIERS!

Life pressures and even people can lead to feelings of isolation. When you are left out of social gatherings or family events, this can lead to a feeling of a lack of self-worth. Maybe you went through a negative relationship in which you suffered from a lack of intimacy. Perhaps you were dismissed by family members over past mistakes, or you were ignored. When you are made to feel erased, it can open the doors for the devil to creep in and try to take over your thoughts. You are valued and have purpose. You are important. You are enough—but not perfect. Here are some ways you can take solace in knowing that you are a child of God.

1. His grace covers you. You will and do make mistakes. You will fall short of your personal goals. On the other side, you will also experience wins. But in those times of defeat, you must be aware that His grace is enough for you and that, in turn, you are also enough. The Lord can strengthen you in your limitations. "For from his fullness we have all received, grace upon grace" (John 1:16).
2. You have purpose. God did not allow His Son to die on a cross for your sins for nothing. He has a plan for you. If you don't know what this is yet, then be patient and continue to seek His will in your life. If you do know your purpose, then glorify the Lord in all you do. "And we know that for those who love God all things work together for good, for those who are called according to his purpose" (Romans 8:28).

3. You have a heavenly Father. Your worth is not defined by your job or relationships or failures or accomplishments. Being appreciated by your coworkers or family and friends is nice but not needed to determine your worth to the Lord.

4. You are loved. God loves you. He will never leave or forsake you and wants the best for you. All you need to do is honor and worship Him to the best of your ability and serve Him with all of your might and strength. "Draw near to God, and he will draw near to you. Cleanse your hands, you sinners, and purify your hearts, you double-minded" (James 4:8).

5. You are forgiven and can lead a wonderful life. When people or circumstances pile up on you, know that you are forgiven or can ask for forgiveness. This won't whitewash your past, but it will cover your sins in the blood of Christ. That's what is the most important thing.

Mendoza was snubbed by some college football programs and was listed as a two-star recruit. Many of those programs who passed on him probably regret their decision not to take him more seriously or give him a shot. But he stayed focused and worked hard for those who did believe in him. God believes in you, and He is on your side.

DAY 24

JUST TRUST

January 19, 2026: Indiana 27, Miami 21

CFP National Championship

Let not your hearts be troubled. Believe in God; believe also in me.

—John 14:1

With less than ten minutes to go in the College Football Playoffs National Championship game, No. 1 Indiana had the ball on the twelve-yard line on fourth down with five yards to go for the first down and was clinging to a 17–14 lead.

There was no hesitation by head coach, Curt Cignetti—you go for the touchdown. A field goal meant giving up. "The coverage before—they were in the coverage where that play would work," he told ESPN after the game. "We put it in for this game. It's quarterback draw but it was blocked differently. And we rolled the dice and said they're going to be in it again and they were and we blocked it well and he broke a tackle or two and got in the end zone."[21]

Indiana quarterback Fernando Mendoza had a run for the ages. The Heisman Trophy winner jumped over one of his own linemen and ran away from two Miami Hurricane defenders. Then he miraculously kept his balance and spun back toward the end zone and dove into the air with the ball extended and crossed the goal line. As he was horizontal and still in the air, Mendoza took a brutal hit from a Hurricane defender but held on to the ball.

The "epic" run, as *Sports Illustrated* described it, gave Indiana a ten-point lead in the fourth quarter and motivated the Hoosiers to hang on to win the school's first ever National Championship. Cignetti said Mendoza had the heart of a lion on that play.

In an article published by IUHoosiers.com, Mendoza said, "I trusted my linemen, and everybody in that entire offense, that entire team had a gritty performance. We were all putting our bodies on the line, so it was the least I could do for my brothers."[22]

---

21 Nick Bromberg, "Fernando Mendoza's Epic Fourth-Down TD Run Powers Indiana to Its First National Title Ever," Yahoo! Sports, January 20, 2026, https://sports.yahoo.com/college-football/breaking-news/live/fernando-mendozas-epic-4th-down-td-run-powers-indiana-to-its-first-national-title-ever-231344237.html?guccounter=1.

22 Pete DiPrimio, "Perfection Punctuates National Title," Indiana University Athletics, January 20, 2026, https://iuhoosiers.com/news/2026/1/20/football-cfp-ncg-recap-PETE.

Some trust in chariots and some in horses,
but we trust in the name of the LORD our God.
—Psalm 20:7

FOR THE CREAM AND CRIMSON

You say you trust the Lord, but do you? Have unanswered prayers or intense personal sufferings caused you to doubt your trust in Christ? Perhaps you are having issues with God because life has not turned out the way you planned. Maybe you struggle financially or have experienced a major health setback or a family tragedy. Maybe someone you looked up to let you down and was involved in a scandal that left you frustrated. Perhaps the conflict in the world has caused you anger and confusion.

HOO-HOO-HOO-HOOSIERS!

You, as a believer in the Lord, should and must trust in God in all circumstances. God is omniscient, loving, and faithful. Can you say that about yourself? The Lord works all things out even if you don't see how or understand. He is the firm foundation and is unchanged. When times get tough, you must trust Him. In the darkest hour, you have to rely on His promises to you. When you hear words that cause pain at crucial times, that is when you turn it over to Him. Here are some reasons you can *always* trust God.

1. He is faithful. Even when you are not, he is consistent and true. He will deliver you at the appropriate

time. Trust Him. "But the Lord is faithful. He will establish you and guard you against the evil one" (2 Thessalonians 3:3).

2. His plan is wise. You do not know the future, but He does. You may not understand what's going on at the time, but He does. His plan is perfect. There are times you'd like to be let in on the secret, but you are not. Trust Him. "O Lord, how manifold are your works! / In wisdom have you made them all; / the earth is full of your creatures" (Psalm 104:24).

3. His love is unconditional. This brings you peace and comfort when faced with lousy circumstances. When times get tough, know that His love makes it all better. Trust Him. "Anyone who does not love does not know God, because God is love" (1 John 4:8).

4. He has the power. He can make all things new and solve your problem for you. Thank Him before He does, and always thank Him after. Praise Him in the storm, and after. Trust Him. "The Lord passed before him and proclaimed, 'The Lord, the Lord, a God merciful and gracious, slow to anger, and abounding in steadfast love and faithfulness" (Exodus 34:6).

5. He will overcome fear. When you put your faith in Him, all the fear disappears. You are told not to worry, but you do because you are human. Focus on prayer and don't try to solve the problem all by yourself. It's OK to be active, just don't take over. Trust Him. "There is no

> fear in love, but perfect love casts out fear. For fear has to do with punishment, and whoever fears has not been perfected in love" (1 John 4:18).

Mendoza said he trusted his linemen in his "epic" run that will be forever called "The Dive." He had to. They were all he had. The same goes for you. Trust God because, really, He is all you have.

DAY 25

MAKE THE PLAY

January 19, 2026: Indiana 27, Miami 21

CFP National Championship

Do not neglect to do good and to share what you have, for such sacrifices are pleasing to God.

—Hebrews 13:16

With about a minute to go in the CFP National Championship, the Indiana Hoosiers needed someone to make a play. The Miami Hurricanes were in Hoosier territory and needed a touchdown.

Trailing 27–21 with less than one minute remaining on the game clock, Miami quarterback Carson Beck dropped back to pass, looked left, and fired from about the IU forty-eight-yard line toward receiver Keelan Marion down the sideline.

It was time.

Indiana defensive back Jamari Sharpe tracked the ball in flight, jumped up, and snagged the pass to secure the win for the Hoosiers. In an article in *Sports Illustrated*, "Sharpe took a knee, then rose from the grass and sprinted to the endzone, where teammates hurried after him to jumpstart a national championship celebration Indiana once thought impossible."[23]

The Indiana Hoosiers stayed undefeated at 16–0 for the first time and won the National Championship—for the first time. And they did it in Miami's backyard at Hard Rock Stadium in Miami Gardens, Florida.

For Sharpe, a Florida native, the moment was surreal. "This is an amazing feeling," he said in a post published on IUHoosiers.com. "I'm so happy to be in this situation. I'm so proud of my teammates and coaches to make it possible for us to come out and ball."[24]

> *Therefore encourage one another and build one another up, just as you are doing.*
>
> —1 Thessalonians 5:11

FOR THE CREAM AND CRIMSON

Do you want to get in the game of life and have a positive impact on society? Everyone does. But if you have noticed, only a few people go into action. This applies to the old saying that "if you want something done, ask someone who is busy." Perhaps you've been on the sidelines of life and preoccupied with distractions

---

23 Daniel Flick, "Indiana Football's Defense Needed a Play. Jamari Sharpe Made It," *Sports Illustrated*, January 20, 2026, https://www.si.com/college/indiana/football/indiana-football-defense-jamari-sharpe-made-play-cfp-national-championship-love-hoosiers-miami.

24 Pete DiPrimio, "Perfection Punctuates National Title," Indiana University Athletics, January 20, 2026, https://iuhoosiers.com/news/2026/1/20/football-cfp-ncg-recap-PETE.

but are ready to make a difference. What can you do? Keep in mind you don't have to set the world on fire or be in the spotlight. Strive to please the Lord.

HOO-HOO-HOO-HOOSIERS!

The coach calls the defensive play and puts you in the game at a crucial time. He needs you to make a big play. However, in this case, the big moment may not include accolades and fanfare or a national championship. Will you rise up and make the play? Here are some ways you can contribute and help your team win.

1. Visit. Take something that is valuable, like your time, and spend it on others. Visit friends who may be in your local hospital or even those you don't know. Some hospitals allow you to read to children with approval. This is something to ponder. You can also visit people in your hometown who cannot get out and go to church anymore. "Religion that is pure and undefiled before God the Father is this: to visit orphans and widows in their affliction, and to keep oneself unstained from the world" (James 1:27).

2. Run. Become involved in local politics. Find your political organization, attend meetings, and offer to help. The potential is endless. Who knows? You can even run for an office. Your neighborhood and county need principled people in positions of leadership. "First of all, then, I urge that supplications, prayers, intercessions, and thanksgivings be made for all people, for

kings and all who are in high positions, that we may lead a peaceful and quiet life, godly and dignified in every way" (1 Timothy 2:1–2).

3. Volunteer. Find a civic group near to your heart's desires and get active. Simply do an internet search with your town's name followed by "volunteer opportunities" to get ideas. Research the group first to ensure their goals align with yours. "And let our people learn to devote themselves to good works, so as to help cases of urgent need, and not be unfruitful" (Titus 3:14).

4. Organize. Put together a small group of people from your church to help around your community. For example, your group could help with maintenance of a widow's property. You could clean up your neighborhood or lend a hand at a food pantry.

5. Pay. Use your resources for good. Pay for a meal for the people behind you in line. Take some donuts to a hospice nurse unit at night. Do this kind of thing without fanfare or recognition.

> You are the salt of the earth, but if salt has lost its taste, how shall its saltiness be restored? It is no longer good for anything except to be thrown out and trampled under people's feet.
>
> You are the light of the world. A city set on a hill cannot be hidden. Nor do people light a lamp and put it under a basket, but on a stand, and it gives light to all in the house. In the same way, let your light shine before others, so that they may see your

> good works and give glory to your Father who is in heaven (Matthew 5:13–16).

You don't need to make a play on national TV for people to cheer you on. You just have to be in the place God puts you. Jamari Sharpe was in the right place and made the play. As a Christian, you can do the same and glorify Christ through your actions. While works will not get you to heaven, they do make the journey much sweeter.

DAY 26

BE A JUNKIE

Fernando Mendoza

Heisman Trophy Winner

Those who look to him are radiant,
and their faces shall never be ashamed.
—Psalm 34:5

When the 2025 football season at Indiana started, few fans throughout the nation knew who Fernando Mendoza was. But by the time his Hoosiers won the CFP National Championship, he was a household name.

He guided Indiana to the first ever 16–0 season and the first ever CFP National Championship in the school's football history. The redshirt junior did it all.

He won a CFP National Championship.

He was named the CFP National Championship Game Offensive MVP.

He won the prestigious Heisman Trophy.

He won the Walter Camp Award.

He won the Maxwell Award.

He was named the AP College Football Player of the Year.

He won the Davey O'Brien Award.

He won the Manning Award.

He was a consensus all-American player.

He was named the Big Ten Most Valuable Player.

He won the Big Ten Championship Game.

He was named the Big Ten Championship Game MVP.

And there were other accolades.

But fans will always remember him for his gutsy performances in the clutch that led to victory over No. 1-ranked Ohio State for the Big Ten Championship, and then how he ran the tables for the CFP National Championship and eventually the huge win over Miami for it all.

Indiana's first Heisman Trophy winner is known for his high football IQ and his rhythm-based pocket style. He is a self-professed "football junkie," which means he spends hours watching film and trying to improve his craft. He loves to study film and will prepare physically and mentally for hours before the next game.

What are your characteristics as a believer?

Stay dressed for action and keep your lamps burning.

—Luke 12:35

FOR THE CREAM AND CRIMSON

If you had to describe yourself in a job interview or on a Christian-based dating application, how would you do that? What words would come to mind? There would be several common ones to choose from, such as *honest*, *dependable*, *forgiven*, *humble*, *fun*, *daring*, *compulsive*, *biblical*, *selfish*, *charitable*, *talkative*, *quiet*, *reserved*, *outgoing*. But how about *junkie*?

HOO-HOO-HOO-HOOSIERS!

If you are a "junkie for Christ," that is a nonliteral expression that implies you are addicted to the Lord and His teachings. That might be a great way to describe yourself if it's an accurate depiction. If you are addicted to or a junkie for the Lord, then you are obsessed with His power to transform lives, especially yours. Here are some ways to cultivate your addiction to the Savior.

1. Immerse yourself in the Bible. Fernando likes to watch game film of his opponents and know their weaknesses and strengths. You can do the same by studying God's Word and knowing the playbook. He has prepared for you. "Open my eyes, that I may behold / wondrous things out of your law" (Psalm 119:18).

2. Have a deep hunger for spiritual practice. Pray. Read. Attend. Those are the fundamentals of a winning Christian. Talk to Christ, pray every day, and thank Him for all He's done for you. Read His love letter to you each day and attend a good church on a regular basis.

3. Choose His will over yours. Listen to your coach. Fernando would not have guided his team to wins

unless he listened to the instructions from his coaches. You have to do the same. Listen in prayer to the Holy Spirit and also take into consideration what your church leaders and small group or Sunday school teachers instruct. "Your kingdom come, / your will be done, / on earth as it is in heaven" (Matthew 6:10).

4. Put your needs last. Put others first. What your family needs takes priority over yours. Give back to your community.

5. Focus on God's glory first. When you put Him at the center of your life, then the accolades might begin to come in. That is not why you strive to be the best, but it might be a good bonus. If it happens, give God the glory, and if it doesn't, still give God the glory. "Be exalted, O Lord, in your strength! / We will sing and praise your power" (Psalm 21:13).

Strive to be like Fernando Mendoza in the sense that he is a "junkie." Be obsessed with the Scriptures and fall in love with going to church to celebrate the King of kings. If you are remembered for being the best witness for Christ, then that will be better than winning a national championship.

DAY 27

A JUST-WIN ATTITUDE

Coach Curt Cignetti

Coach of the Year

For the LORD *your God is he who goes with you to fight for you against your enemies, to give you the victory.*
—Deuteronomy 20:4

Without a doubt, Curt Cignetti transformed the Indiana University football program.

In the past, when you thought of IU, you thought of an iconic basketball powerhouse and about coaching legend Bobby Knight. But within just two short years, Cignetti made football at Indiana relevant. In those two seasons, he propelled the Hoosiers to a Big Ten Championship and a CFP National Championship—both firsts for the university.

How did he do this?

The answer is simple: through attitude. Cignetti encouraged and demanded an immediate cultural change in overall attitude. He changed the psychology of a losing program and instilled "swagger" and "confidence" not only for his players, but for the entire sports program.

And the results spoke for themselves. In two seasons, he emphasized discipline, efficiency, and execution. He rebuilt the entire team roster and took advantage of transfer portal opportunities to bring in his style of player.

Cignetti wanted character over talent and coachability over playmakers. He said from the get-go that he got results and just won games—period.

Now fans expect the Hoosiers to win on the football field as well as the basketball court. Mission accomplished: Indiana football is for real.

Are you a positive Christian?

> *But thanks be to God, who gives us the victory through our Lord Jesus Christ.*
>
> —1 Corinthians 15:57

FOR THE CREAM AND CRIMSON

Do others want what you have? Does your Christian witness and attitude attract others? Or are you a negative believer who is prone to be a doom-and-gloomer? Do you exude a positive demeanor that makes people want to know more about Jesus? Or do you maintain a blah personality? Attitude is something you can control, and it can be the difference in winning and losing.

HOO-HOO-HOO-HOOSIERS!

You need to be a positive Christian for many reasons. For one, you are on the winning side. What better reason? Big advantages include a deeper and lasting inner peace and joy. When you are positive, you reduce anxiety and have a better chance at a lasting relationship with others. It's about a faith-driven mindset that God is all you need. Here are some other benefits to maintaining a positive Christian attitude.

1. You have improved mental health and well-being. When you have hope, faith, and an optimistic outlook, your mental health is stronger. And why should you not be optimistic? You win in the end. "For God gave us a spirit not of fear but of power and love and self-control" (2 Timothy 1:7).

2. You have a positive perspective. This will help you see the overall picture, especially during times of struggles. You can overcome challenges by trusting in God's strength and rely on Him instead of focusing on the negative. "This is the day that the LORD has made; / let us rejoice and be glad in it" (Psalm 118:24).

3. Your guilt is gone. This allows you to look at the liberation God provides when He forgives you of your past. There may be consequences to deal with, but He can take away your guilt and shame. And that's a big one. "There is therefore now no condemnation for those who are in Christ Jesus" (Romans 8:1).

4. You have a stable character. When you delve into the Scriptures, it will help you stay grounded and portray the kind of person whom you want to be and whom you

want others to see. You will find yourself staying away from negative trends, especially on social media.

5. Your hope is stronger. With God on your side, you will act with a sense of purpose and calling because you have one. You have eternal life and a real purpose to share the good news of Christ. Hope is a powerful work and can lift the spirits of those around you once everyone sees it in you. "Rejoice in hope, be patient in tribulation, be constant in prayer" (Romans 12:12).

Coach Cignetti brought the change in attitude from a losing program to one of winning. The team catapulted to the top instantly because they thought they could. You must be the same. Your positive Christian attitude will attract others, especially those who need to be encouraged. Be that bright light of hope to a dark world and just win.

DAY 28

WHO INSPIRES YOU?

Elsa Mendoza

Fernando Mendoza's Mother

Love is patient and kind; love does not envy or boast; it is not arrogant or rude. It does not insist on its own way; it is not irritable or resentful; it does not rejoice at wrongdoing, but rejoices with the truth. Love bears all things, believes all things, hopes all things, endures all things.

—1 Corinthians 13:4–7

The 2025–26 season for the Indiana Hoosiers was memorable in many ways. A Big Ten Championship coupled with a CFP National Championship and an undefeated season (16–0) topped the charts.

Quarterback Fernando Mendoza was also remarkable. He threw for 3,535 yards with forty-one touchdowns and only six interceptions. He won the prestigious Heisman Trophy, had a completion rate of 72 percent, and tossed in seven rushing touchdowns. He credits his head coach and team for the winning attitude but gives his mother, Elsa, accolades for the inspiration to be a better person.

According to an article published in *USA Today*, Elsa Mendoza is a former tennis player from the University of Miami. She is the best fan of her son and her entire family while she battles multiple sclerosis.

Fernando Mendoza said, "Our mom is our inspiration, our light, and gives us positivity every single day. . . . She's my idol. I know she's the same for Alberto, as both of our parents are, and seeing her fight and fight every single day gives us no excuse to ever take anything for granted."

The article continued,

> Fernando Mendoza shared that his mom has a tough time "moving around" at this point in her battle. She was in Indianapolis at Lucas Oil Stadium for the Big Ten Championship game and was seen in a wheelchair. "At this point, she has a tough time moving around and stuff like that, but her happiness, her joy and her determination is what inspires me every single day and that's what pushes me," Fernando told Hoosiers Connect. "You know, if I'm in a workout and I'm feeling tired, you know, a little thought in my mind goes, 'Maybe you should skip out on this set' or something like that, I'll be like, my mom is out here every single day putting a ton of work, a ton of dedication and still with a great attitude, a great positive attitude in everything she does."[25]

---

25 John Leuzzi, "Fernando Mendoza's Mom Is Heisman Winner's Best Friend, Inspiration," *USA Today*, January 19, 2026, https://www.usatoday.com/story/sports/ncaaf/bigten/2026/01/19/fernando-mendoza-mom-elsa-wheelchair-ms-multiple-sclerosis-indiana-football-national-championship/87720841007/.

Who inspires you to be a better person? Do you return the favor and motivate anyone?

The steadfast love of the L*ORD never ceases;*
his mercies never come to an end;
they are new every morning;
great is your faithfulness.
—Lamentations 3:22–23

FOR THE CREAM AND CRIMSON

Who do you draw inspiration from when times get tough? Have you had moments when you wanted to give up on a quest or a task? Have you ever thought about just tossing in the towel on something you've been working toward because of a lack of progress? Do you reach out to anyone? Do you find inspiration from someone in your life? Do you provide any source of motivation for a loved one?

HOO-HOO-HOO-HOOSIERS!

You can be a light to someone in a dark world. And it doesn't take much either. You can inspire those around you with little actions like a smile or a positive attitude. You can demonstrate Christ's love in your life by intentional acts of kindness. It's easy to complain about situations and circumstances, but take a look at how Elsa deals with life. She encourages and inspires. Here are some ways you can do the same.

1. Give intentional encouragement. Look for opportunities to inspire and lift up others in gloomy situations. Be cautious not to be pushy but to do it with love and tenderness. Try to understand situations with friends or family who are struggling and let them know they are loved without conditions. "Do nothing from selfish ambition or conceit, but in humility count others more significant than yourselves" (Philippians 2:3).

2. Be joyful and generous. Give with a joyous heart and attitude. If you can't give your time and money without a song in your heart, you should pray about your attitude. Prepare a meal for someone or give your time and visit people who are not as blessed as you. Run an errand for an elderly person or cut the grass for a neighbor who is pressed for time. "Give, and it will be given to you. Good measure, pressed down, shaken together, running over, will be put into your lap. For with the measure you use it will be measured back to you" (Luke 6:38).

3. Remember that positivity is contagious. If you show the love of Christ in all situations and stay positive, it will carry over onto others in your life. Battles will happen, and you will lose a fight or two, but when you look at the big picture and how much God loves you, then your outlook will change. The moment may not be what you want, but the Lord is enough. Let everyone see that, and it will inspire them.

4. Share with others. You can inspire someone by sharing your story. It doesn't have to be a dramatic transformational story, but it's yours. Be open about your own struggles and how God is guiding you, which helps others feel less alone and encourages their own growth. "But if you warn the wicked to turn from his way, and he does not turn from his way, that person shall die in his iniquity, but you will have delivered your soul" (Ezekiel 33:9).

5. Foster unity. You can act as a bridge builder and encourage unity and growth in faith. You can be the person who inspires unity instead of division. Never compromise your own convictions, but strive to work with others. Reach out and be the one. "With all humility and gentleness, with patience, bearing with one another in love, eager to maintain the unity of the Spirit in the bond of peace" (Ephesians 4:2–3).

Fernando is inspired by his mother, who battles MS and does it with a smile. She makes the most of her situation and knows God is in control. You can do the same for people in your life. If you have a condition that limits your ability, be an inspiration. If you are blessed not to have one, then be an inspiration. The point here is to be a positive light in a dark world.

DAY 29

THE MAGNIFICENT 7

How Fellowship Helps

Finally, all of you, have unity of mind, sympathy, brotherly love, a tender heart, and a humble mind.

—1 Peter 3:8

When Indiana head coach Curt Cignetti came to Bloomington, several of his players followed.

In 2024, Cignetti left James Madison University to lead the Hoosiers, a football program limping through the NCAA. He rebuilt and reenergized IU from the depths of despair into an undefeated, 16–0 season in 2025, a No. 1 ranking, a Big Ten Championship, and a CFP National Championship. Originally, thirteen players followed Cignetti from JMU. Of those thirteen, seven helped to form a nucleus of solidarity.

Those players were D'Angelo Ponds, a defensive back; Solomon Vanhorse, a running back; Tyrique Tucker, an defensive lineman; Elijah Sarratt, a wide receiver; Kaelon Black, a running back; Aiden Fisher, a linebacker; and Mikail Kamara, a defensive lineman. This little group of misfits bonded and helped form the team that demolished every opponent on their way to the national title.

In an article on CBS Sports, Fisher said the move to Indiana was a lifesaver. "I know for me, it changed my life. I'm here playing at the highest level with some guys that I was playing at a very small level at, and it's just been a crazy journey and one that I'm so glad that we got to do together."[26]

Cignetti, in the article, said the seven players brought leadership and stability to the program. "They had that championship attitude. They were able to answer questions for the guys to decide to return, and the right guys returned. I think that accelerated our development as a program, there's no question about it."[27]

Working together is vital and forms a strong bond.

Show hospitality to one another without grumbling.

—1 Peter 4:9

FOR THE CREAM AND CRIMSON

Do you have a group of friends who will follow and help you? Are there a few people in your circle you trust? Or are you a loner with only one or two people you count on for enjoyment or fellowship? If you are fortunate enough to have a friend to lean on, then you are blessed. But do you find it important to have more people in your circle?

---

26 Shehan Jeyarajah, "Indiana's Magnificent Seven: The James Madison Transfers Who Built a Champion," CBS Sports, January 20, 2026, https://www.cbssports.com/college-football/news/indianas-national-title-was-built-by-seven-jmu-transfers/.

27 Jeyarajah, "Indiana's Magnificent Seven."

HOO-HOO-HOO-HOOSIERS!

Christian fellowship is essential for your spiritual growth. It's important for encouragement, emotional support, and a community to do life with. On the other end, it helps to combat the increasing problem of isolation and offers accountability. Life is better if it's shared. You may enjoy your moments of alone time—and that's important, too, at times—but when you surround yourself with like-minded people, it will help to build your faith. Here are some key aspects of strong fellowship.

1. Spiritual growth. Indiana would not have won if they depended on only one or two players. They needed everyone. Other believers in your life will only help you get better. Strive to help one another be like Jesus. "Be imitators of me, as I am of Christ" (1 Corinthians 11:1).

2. Encouragement. This will help you avoid loneliness and times of discouragement. "You keep him in perfect peace / whose mind is stayed on you, / because he trusts in you" (Isaiah 26:3).

3. Accountability. You need this as much as you need your friends. If you are alone, the devil will blitz you when you are not expecting it and sack you for a loss. You need an offensive line and friends who will block.

4. Learning from one another. Suggestions and advice are important in life. Making a mistake is expected, and learning a lesson is a must. Bounce ideas off one another.

5. Fun. Take trips; do life together. Be open and honest and have a group of people whom you trust. "His master said to him, 'Well done, good and faithful servant. You have been faithful over a little; I will set you over much. Enter into the joy of your master'" (Matthew 25:21).

No one likes to be alone. Life is meant to be shared and enjoyed. It's better with a group of people.

DAY 30

JUST KEEP WORKING

Omar Cooper Jr.

Indiana Wide Receiver

Jesus Christ is the same yesterday and today and forever.
—Hebrews 13:8

Life happens. Change happens. Just ask Indiana wide receiver Omar Cooper Jr.

The standout ball catcher had a big decision to make when Tom Allen was fired as the head coach of the Indiana Hoosier football program. Curt Cignetti came in to rebuild the program, and most of the roster departed. But not Cooper.

The Indianapolis native from Lawrence North High School saw the big picture, worked hard on his craft, and made the decision to stay home. He had a new coach, a new team, a new perspective, and a new attitude. In the end, he made the right decision.

Cooper was a major contributor to a team that went 16–0, won the Big Ten Championship, and won the first ever CFP National Championship. He kept his work ethic, and it paid off.

The redshirt junior hauled in 937 yards and had thirteen touchdowns during the historic championship run.

"From freshman year to now, you never know what can happen," Cooper said in an article on TheHoosier.com. "You just gotta stay down, keep your head down and just keep working."[28]

A lot can change in the course of a few days, weeks, months, and years. But through it all, God never changes.

> *For I know the plans I have for you, declares the Lord, plans for welfare and not for evil, to give you a future and a hope.*
>
> —Jeremiah 29:11

FOR THE CREAM AND CRIMSON

One thing in life is certain: It will change. You may be on top of the world one minute and in a valley the next. Your career can end in a moment through a firing, a relocation, or a retirement. Your relationship might fall apart unexpectedly through a divorce, having children, experiencing the empty-nest syndrome, or death. You could move to a new location or suffer a significant health issue or undergo a life-changing sickness.

---

28 Colin McMahon, "Omar Cooper Jr. Believed in Himself. Now He's One of the Top Prospects in the 2026 NFL Draft," *The Hoosier*, February 28, 2026, https://www.on3.com/teams/indiana-hoosiers/news/omar-cooper-jr-believed-in-himself-now-hes-one-of-the-top-prospects-in-the-2026-nfl-draft/.

HOO-HOO-HOO-HOOSIERS!

You can try your best to navigate these changes. You can certainly overcome some of the little ones by yourself. But how do you handle the big ones? The huge decisions or circumstances out of your control? Do you leave for the greener grass, or do you stick it out to see what happens? Do you rely on the Lord for His guidance? Do you consider His will in your life, or do you just make the decision? Life will throw some important changes at you. Here are some ways to handle those changes.

1. Accept the challenge. If you resist change, it may just get the better of you. Instead, look at it as an opportunity to develop character and a way to grow as a believer.

2. Embrace His grace. It's free. Be patient and let the Lord work in your life. Don't get in a rush for results. Instead, be excited for what the Lord will show you and reveal to you in the unknown journey. "For you shall go out in joy / and be led forth in peace; / the mountains and the hills before you / shall break forth into singing, / and all the trees of the field shall clap their hands" (Isaiah 55:12).

3. Find comfort in Scripture. Find those accounts of joy and happiness and peace and dwell in them for a while. Dive deep into the Psalms or see how the Lord provided for the children of Israel and even Job. "Let your steadfast love comfort me / according to your promise to your servant" (Psalm 119:76).

4. Practice gratitude. Find the good in your situation and look for the positive. Be thankful for the problems and anticipate the good that will come out of any decision you make for God. "For where your treasure is, there your heart will be also" (Matthew 6:21).

5. Leverage community. Talk to church leaders and friends who have gone through similar situations. Learn how they depended on the Lord for wisdom and discernment. It's a good idea to gather opinions from those who have experience.

Cooper made the decision to stay at Indiana. He didn't take it lightly, but it worked out for everyone involved. You can do the same. Take your time, weigh the pros and cons, and listen to His advice for you. You can't go wrong.

ABOUT THE AUTHOR

Del Duduit is an award-winning author and sportswriter who has covered major sporting events including the Super Bowl and the Indianapolis 500. His work has appeared in *Sports Spectrum*, *Clubhouse Magazine*, *Decision Magazine*, *Athletes in Action*, and the *Western Journal* in addition to several other publications. Del has taught several writing classes with Serious Writer, Inc. and given instructional courses in Italy as well. He has appeared on many television shows and podcasts, instructed sports journalism classes at the college level, and won several awards as a full-time sportswriter. He lives in Southern Ohio with his wife, Angie.

www.ingramcontent.com/pod-product-compliance
Lightning Source LLC
Chambersburg PA
CBHW070244130726
48054CB00021B/137

* 9 7 8 1 5 6 3 0 9 8 1 3 0 *